THE BIG THREE AT YALTA, FEBRUARY, 1945

Prime Minister Churchill, President Roosevelt, and Premier Stalin.

THE NEW DEAL AND WORLD AFFAIRS

A CHRONICLE OF
INTERNATIONAL AFFAIRS, 1933–1945
BY ALLAN NEVINS

NEW HAVEN: YALE UNIVERSITY PRESS
TORONTO: GLASGOW, BROOK & CO.
LONDON: GEOFFREY CUMBERLEGE
OXFORD UNIVERSITY PRESS
1950

CONTENTS

ILLUSTRATION

THE BIG THREE AT YALTA, FEBRUARY, 1945
    Prime Minister Churchill, President Roosevelt,
    and Premier Stalin. International News Photo.   *Frontispiece*

THE NEW DEAL

AND WORLD AFFAIRS

∵

CHAPTER I

THE NEW DEAL AND THE LONDON CONFERENCE

THE election of Franklin D. Roosevelt in the fall of 1932 brought about far less change of front in international than in domestic policies. For one reason, President Hoover and Secretary Stimson had in many respects followed a liberal and progressive path which would simply have to be continued. Hoover's proposal for a moratorium on reparations and war debts, Stimson's readiness for a firm cooperation with the League during the Manchurian crisis, and their active measures to promote world disarmament had all indicated a realization of the importance of American aid to other powers in meeting the political and economic problems of the day. Hoover's good neighbor policy toward Latin America could not be abandoned. For another reason, the Democratic party no less than the Republican had its large body of isolationists. Under pressure from William Randolph Hearst, Roosevelt had announced before his nomination that he did not favor League membership. Two shifts in attitude, and two only, were anticipated. First, the party in general and Cordell Hull in particular had a large inheritance of Wilsonian ideas, which should make for a gradual movement toward broader international activities. Second, the Democrats were committed to a low tariff doctrine which was expected to reduce the economic nationalism so evident under Hoover.

The international situation when Roosevelt took office was ominous in the extreme. Europe as well as America was economically prostrate; all nations were seething with discontent, and in Latin America revolution was active. The Hoover moratorium had expired in June, 1932, and although Britain made a payment in December, France and other countries defaulted on their war debts. Japan was pursuing a course of aggression in the Far East which Stimson believed must inevitably lead to war with the United States. Three weeks after Roosevelt's inauguration (March 27) the Japanese Government, condemned by the League Assembly, announced that it would withdraw from the League after the required two-year interval. Hitler by the elections of March 5 became German

Chancellor, and before the end of the month was given dictatorial powers; he was already planning the persecution of the Jews and the suppression of rival parties. Disorder, fear, aggression, were all prominent in the world scene.

Some weeks before March 4, 1933, it was known that Senator Cordell Hull would be the new Secretary of State, and the announcement delighted those who hoped for boldly progressive policies. The sixty-three-year-old Tennesseean, who had come of militant mountaineer stock, was a man of rugged convictions, certain to insist on a strong hand in shaping the nation's course. A wise veteran of House and Senate, he had a host of friends in both bodies. From his days as a Captain in the Spanish-American War, he had given close attention to foreign affairs, while from Grover Cleveland's time he had been interested in tariff reduction as part of a program of liberal reform. Wilson's battle for the League had enlisted his fervent adherence, and as Chairman of the Democratic National Committee in the 1920's he had tried to keep the party true to Wilsonian principles. Though, like Hughes and Stimson, as Secretary he kept out of politics and labored to enlist bipartisan support, he was ready to rally public sentiment for his aims. If necessary, he "went a-feudin' " like his father, who had tracked down and slain a Civil War guerrilla who tried to assassinate him.

For twelve years the relations between Hull and Roosevelt were destined to exhibit unbroken harmony. It was necessary for the President, however, to take account of a far wider range of issues than for Hull. He employed in foreign affairs various Departments, especially the Treasury under Henry Morgenthau, Jr., special agencies like the Board of Economic Warfare under Henry Wallace, and such individuals as Harry Hopkins, a social worker of keen mind who held various posts of importance; with the result that Hull sometimes felt his authority ignored. The President frequently had to consult expediency, whereas Hull always clung to principle. At all times the Secretary showed a steadfast, dogged type of statesmanship. He was endlessly patient. When he became exasperated with Secretary Wallace's encroachments on his field, and took steps to end the intrusion, they were not violent. "I used old-fashioned methods," he told James A. Farley. "I gave him plenty of rope." But in dealing with the complex, murky foreign situation, the President's vision often pierced further into the future; his imagination, resiliency, and resourcefulness sometimes conquered difficulties that defied Hull's blunt weapons; his swift changes of course avoided many a submerged rock. To an increasing extent, therefore, Roosevelt was his own Secretary of State—as most strong Presidents have been. On the maintenance of world order the two men saw eye to eye, for they had the same detestation of dictatorships and aggression. Despite his lukewarm campaign utterances, Roosevelt was friendly to the League; but unlike Hull, the President was by no means a convinced internationalist in the economic field. Roosevelt's impetuosity sometimes troubled the Secretary. On the other hand, the President was distressed by the ineffective organization of the State Department, by Hull's tendency to center his energy on his trade-treaty program, and by the cool relations between Hull on one side, and Secretaries Morgenthau and Wallace on the other. In brief, while the two acted in general harmony, their outlook and methods showed sharp divergences.

More than ever before, the State Department under Hull was a hard-working center of manifold activities. He found a generally experienced group of career men, the more notable including Jay P. Moffat, entrusted with western European affairs; James C. Dunn, who dealt at first with protocol and conferences and later with broader problems; S. K. Hornbeck, specialist in Far Eastern affairs; and Herbert Feis, adviser in economic matters. With his first Under-Secretary of State, William Phillips, Hull cooperated admirably; with his second, the able Sumner Welles, his relations gradually became strained; with his third, E. R. Stettinius, he again acted amicably. The President sorely tried

Hull's patience by appointing Raymond Moley as Assistant Secretary of State, for Moley urged economic and political nationalism as the road out of the depression. Fortunately for harmony, the young man's public career was short. The Secretary worked long hours seven days a week, and his staff toiled with equal energy. Year by year foreign affairs grew more complex, exigent, and perilous.

During the interregnum between Roosevelt's election and his inauguration, futile efforts were made to provide for joint action by him and President Hoover. At one point Roosevelt did lend support to the outgoing Administration, for he endorsed the Hoover-Stimson policy of non-recognition in Manchuria. On war debts, armaments, and the preliminary work for the forthcoming World Economic Conference, however, no agreement was reached. Hoover proposed on December 17, 1933, that these interlocked questions be given "coordinate consideration" by a group of American delegates authorized to deal with all three. Roosevelt rejected the idea, saying that the three topics required separate consideration, that the regular diplomatic service could deal with war debts, and that he would not accept responsibility when he lacked joint power. To what extent Roosevelt would revive Wilsonian principles was still not clear. During the campaign he had declared that the Smoot-Hawley Tariff was largely responsible for the continuance of the depression, for it had spurred other lands to frenzied measures of self-containment, accentuated the prostration of world trade, and helped force various countries off the gold standard. However, his attention was focused chiefly upon the domestic crisis. Definite measures to meet the home emergency might not conflict with the international program—but if they did, they would get priority.

On British initiative, tentative arrangements had been made in 1932 for a world economic conference in London, and to this Roosevelt turned immediately after taking office. Preparatory meetings under League auspices had been held at Geneva, and an elaborate program drawn up. To explore the ideas of other nations, the President invited eleven of them to send special representatives *seriatim* to Washington. They arrived in April and May, 1933. Ramsay MacDonald himself brought a British delegation. Other Governments were meanwhile consulted through their diplomatic representatives. All nations, MacDonald pointed out, would enter the conference with free hands. While many topics were discussed, no general agreement was reached, and two of the most vital problems, the war debts and stabilization of currencies, were left quite nebulous. The United States went partially off the gold standard in April; and so many foreign critics declared that the Government had devalued the dollar to gain a stronger trading position at the Economic Conference that Hull sent a specific disclaimer to the four principal American Embassies in Europe.

On May 31, Secretary Hull sailed for London as head of an American delegation which Roosevelt had appointed without due regard to unity. Former Governor James M. Cox of Ohio possessed great ability and earnestness, but no special expertness. Senator Key Pittman of Nevada, chosen because he was Chairman of the Foreign Relations Committee, was a semi-isolationist who believed in high tariffs and whose chief desire was to do something for silver; Senator James Couzens, a Michigan Republican, held unorthodox and even radical financial views. The ideas of Representative Samuel D. McReynolds of Tennessee and Ralph W. Morrison, a retired banker and cotton merchant of Texas, neither an expert, were vague. Raymond Moley, though not a delegate, had been given charge of the preparation of data, and just before the Conference began he delivered a speech belittling the reduction of tariff and other trade barriers, which was the goal closest to Hull's heart. Altogether, great confusion attended the preliminaries of the gathering.

On June 12, with representatives of all important nations in attendance, the Conference was opened by King George V. The sterling group headed by Britain and the gold bloc led by France, Italy, and Poland were ready to act in fair harmony. Four great problems presented themselves. One was overproduction or underconsumption. Another was the unstabilized currencies of the world, subject to violent fluctuations which made trade a perpetual gamble. A third lay in the high tariff walls. The fourth problem, the war debts, was the dark topic which half the delegates regarded as paramount but dared not mention. The whole made up a tangled skein and, among informed Americans, hope for the Conference did not really run high. They knew that the United States and Great Britain would not return to the gold standard, as France wanted them to do; that no nation was yet prepared to reduce its tariffs very sharply; that Germany, Japan, and other countries were unwilling to do away with exchange restrictions; and that war debts would be kept rigidly off the agenda.

In his opening speech Prime Minister MacDonald brought out King Charles's head. While the debts could not be debated in the Conference, he remarked, debated somewhere they would have to be, for they were an obstacle to general recovery. Other nations chorused their assent, Benes and Smuts making emphatic pleas for a prompt settlement. This disconcerted the American delegates. When MacDonald spoke, he knew that next day the British Government would inform the State Department that in place of nearly $76,000,-000 due that month it would make a token payment of but $10,000,000. Italy, Czechoslovakia, and Rumania also made small token payments, while France, Belgium, Poland, and Yugoslavia sent not a farthing. Out of $143,600,000 due at the time, only $11,370,000 was paid.

Debts excluded, the major question before the Conference was the halting of currency fluctuations. Could America, Britain, and France agree on some principle of monetary policy? The French, having come through the wringer with a reduction of the franc to one-fifth of its old worth, were now determined to cling to the gold standard. With them clustered the Italians, Swiss, Belgians, and Dutch. Great Britain wavered between conflicting views; for whereas conservative circles favored a return to the gold standard, many manufacturers and workers favored price-raising by currency management. The MacDonald government was ready to go back to gold, once the price level of goods had been raised sufficiently high to balance costs, and believed that one way to achieve this was to bring the chief currencies of the world into fair balance. Dr. Hjalmar Schacht announced that Germany desired a stable situation in the monetary field.

Everything thus depended upon the United States. If it came out vigorously for stabilization leading to an early general return to the gold standard, this program would almost certainly be carried. The liberal-minded James M. Cox was chosen head of the committee on currency affairs. When he declared that he had always favored "a sound monetary policy," understood the French views, and agreed with Finance Minister Bonnet on the restoration of "financial and monetary order," friends of stabilization were delighted.

But a change had come over the spirit of Roosevelt's dream. Three months had elapsed between his inauguration and the opening of the Conference; the dramatic ninety-nine-day program of recovery and reform was almost completed. Business activity had revived, commodity prices had risen, the stock market had rallied, and the fallen farmer and laborer seemed to be picking themselves from the dust. Much of the credit was no doubt to be given to the psychological rebound encouraged by Roosevelt's own boldness, to the ending of the bank crisis, and to long-term factors operative in business. But it was natural to attribute part of the recovery to dollar devaluation, and to many observers this seemed the decisive factor. The Administration shared the view that a direct relation could be traced between recovery and the decline of the dollar, and it naturally argued that any immediate stabilization would imperil a continuance of the advance. The dollar, Roosevelt reasoned, must be kept free until recovery was assured. He did not reach this conclusion, however, until his delegation had departed for London, and failed to apprise Secretary Hull, ex-Governor Cox, Senator Couzens, Senator Pittman, and others of his change of opinion.

The first two weeks of the Conference, therefore, found the American delegates utterly at sea. They did not know the Administration's mind or their own minds. Dispatches from London reported a gravitation toward stabilization and gold. Cox's statement coincided with the drafting by British and American experts of a tentative plan for holding both dollar and pound at existing levels. The response to these cables was a break in Wall Street. If immediate stabilization were accepted, then the Administration could not make use of the "reflationary" powers lately given it by Congress, and the upward movement in commodities and stocks might cease. Secretary of the Treasury Woodin at once warned the world that Washington had not yet made up its mind. This statement deepened the existing confusion in London, with European delegations calling for light and the American delegates anxiously querying Washington as to its real intentions. In the midst of the perplexity, Raymond Moley, after a dramatic final interview with the President at sea, sailed for the Conference as liaison agent for Roosevelt. He was to bring information of the most recent developments in Washington. The professor *ex machina* was received in London like a king. It was mistakenly assumed that he brought fresh instructions, and his arrival on June 27 threw Hull into a humiliating second-fiddle role, which the Secretary keenly resented.

Moley at once took up the stabilization problem. Thus far the American delegation had handled the problem with caution, issuing a statement on June 22 that it believed temporary stabilization "untimely," for it was convinced that price-raising was the most important contribution possible to world betterment. But European hopes had been raised too high to be dashed by this cold water. Delegates of the gold-standard nations continued to believe that the United States might be argued or cajoled into line, and they received encouragement from Moley's readiness to discuss the subject. The dollar during the conference had behaved erratically, oscillating between 76 and 80 cents in gold. This made the position of the pound untenable and raised the threat of Anglo-American competition in the devaluation of currencies. Georges Bonnet of France and others prepared a declaration in support of the gold standard, which they hoped that the five gold-basis countries, the United States, and Great Britain would all sign. The declaration announced that the five nations would stick to their existing financial system and that the American and British took note of this position, recognized its importance, and, without committing themselves to immediate action, reiterated that the establishment of an international gold standard was their "ultimate objective."

This declaration Moley (acting without Hull's cooperation) sent to Roosevelt with a recommendation that he consider its approval. It reached the President on June 30. Moley exhaled confidence that it would be accepted. Next day came a curt announcement of its rejection, and on July 3 a vigorous message which Roosevelt had drafted on the cruiser *Indianapolis* at sea. Influenced by believers in a controlled dollar, and by the rising evidences of recovery, he would countenance no stabilization policy.

Thus, as Roosevelt confessed later, was the Conference "torpedoed." Moley was completely deflated. Hull told him: "You had better get back home. You had no business here in the first place." European voices rose in a hubbub of angry protest, demanding immediate adjournment. The French press was specially vitriolic. MacDonald, feeling that Roosevelt had repudiated the fair understanding they had reached at Washington that spring, grimly refused to take another step.

On receiving the rejection, Hull was anxious that the onus of disrupting the Conference should not be placed on Roosevelt's shoulders. When the steering committee met on July 6, he calmly seized the rudder to prevent an abrupt adjournment. For a time the delegates lingered in London, while he tried to soothe their feelings, but without accomplishing anything. Though Hull held some valuable talks with European leaders on his plan for reciprocal trade treaties, he was crippled even in this by Roosevelt's announcement on June 9 that he would not send any tariff legislation to the current Congress; and the Conference completely failed to reach any decision on tariffs, quotas, exchange controls, and other impediments to world trade.

Indeed, it was one of the most completely abortive gatherings in modern history. The delegates achieved nothing beyond proposing an agreement on silver made by eight nations specially concerned (Key Pittman's work), drafting a wheat agreement, and adopting some innocuous principles on such matters as the cooperation of general banks. When it was over, European chagrin found vent in general denunciation of the Americans. Unquestionably, Roosevelt deserved great blame for the debacle. He had made insufficient preparation for the Conference; he had appointed an inharmonious and largely inexpert delegation; he had vacillated as to his own purposes; and when he had finally placed domestic recovery above international stabilization, he had done so with excessive abruptness and without candid and tactful explanations. His dispatch of Moley to the scene had placed that official in a cruelly false position, aroused European hopes which were sharply dashed, and given justified offense to Hull. Time proved that Roosevelt's central decision was mistaken; for manipulation of the dollar did little or nothing for American recovery, while constructive action in London might have greatly improved world morale.

Almost simultaneously with the breakdown in London occurred the final collapse of the World Disarmament Conference at Geneva. When the failure to reach any agreement in the first session in 1932 was followed by deadlock in the second session of February, 1933, Ramsay MacDonald stepped in with a British plan for solving all difficulties. He proposed that all European armies be placed on a conscription basis; that each army be kept within a low maximum, proportioned roughly to its population; and that heavy artillery and airplanes be sharply limited. Under this plan Germany would receive a fair equality with other nations. To satisfy the demand of France and the Little Entente for security, all the nations which had signed the Kellogg-Briand Pact should meet in conference to decide on measures to prevent its violation. The plan was to hold good for five years, during which time a better arrangement might be devised. Hitler's Germany, however, refused to listen to the proposal. Demanding still better terms, and declaring that the storm-troopers should not be counted as part of the German army, the Reich threatened a rapid rearmament.

May brought a series of dramatic but unavailing proposals at Geneva. President Roosevelt, anxious to make a contribution, sent a personal appeal to all the Governments to accept the British plan. MacDonald, who had gone to Rome to talk with Mussolini about a formula for combining general security with a possible revision of old treaties, continued his labors. French leaders were insisting upon security before they would accept full German parity, and German leaders were demanding full parity before they would talk about security. On May 11 the German Foreign Minister published an article stating that under certain conditions the Reich would have to add to its armaments; and at this uneasy moment Hitler called the neglected Reichstag to meet on May 16. Thereupon President Roosevelt, in the first of numerous efforts to forestall action by Hitler, attempted to impart new life to the Disarmament Conference. The nations, he asserted, should enter into a definite pact of non-aggression. They should agree,

subject to existing treaties, to send no armed force
of any nature whatever across their frontiers. To
demonstrate their good faith, they should discard
completely all weapons which make an attack
possible, so that defense would automatically become perfect, and every country could rest secure
in its frontiers. The first steps should be taken immediately, and while others were pending, no
country should augment its armaments. Through
Dr. Hjalmar Schacht, who was in Washington,
Roosevelt tried to make it clear to Hitler that the
United States regarded Germany as the sole obstacle to a sound disarmament treaty.

The adroit Hitler, taking his cue, chimed in with
a loud "me too," which meant precisely nothing,
telling the Reichstag that Germany could well
support some of Roosevelt's proposals as a means
of ending the international crisis and restoring
order and prosperity. German rearmament had already proceeded to great lengths in spite of the
treaty limits. Foreign observers had noted that the
production of caterpillar tractors for farm use and
of armor plates had risen *pari passu*; the inference
was that tanks were being assembled. Herman
Goering, as Minister of Aviation, had encouraged
the formation of glider clubs and associations for
"sport aviation." In the summer of 1933, after an
alleged air raid which scattered non-visible Communist pamphlets over Berlin, a contract was

given the Siemens factory in Berlin for 150 airplanes, and it was thought that other firms got similar orders. The pilots were ready, trained in sport and commercial aviation. Small arms were soon pouring out in a flood. Germany was once more the world's greatest producer of chemicals, and the I. G. Farbenindustrie was making profitable contacts with foreign firms, including some in the United States, for the exchange of information. Hitler had appointed the coal-and-steel magnate Fritz Thyssen to supreme control over the industries of western Germany. In all German universities, professors of military science had been appointed.

The Roosevelt Administration did not fail to follow up its plan. France had been protesting, like other countries, that even if the League undertook to punish an aggressor American abstention or opposition might defeat its efforts. Our delegation at Geneva was now ready to meet this objection. On May 22, the Chairman, Norman H. Davis, not only reiterated American readiness to accept the British plan, but went on to announce a bold new policy. If a substantial reduction of armaments was effected by general agreement, Washington would contribute in other ways to guarantee the peace. It would consult with other nations, whenever peace was threatened, upon the best means of avoiding a conflict. Moreover, if this international conference determined that a state had breached the peace, and took repressive measures, then the United States, if it concurred in the judgment, would refrain from any action tending to defeat this collective repression.

While the United States had never before gone so far in pledging unity with the League in condemnation of an aggressor, the program now announced was a purely passive policy. America would not hinder the application of collective security, but neither would it promise to help. The Senate Foreign Relations Committee underlined the nation's negative attitude when, a few days after Davis spoke, it rejected a plan proposed in Congress which would have authorized the President to declare an arms embargo against *any* warlike country. Instead, it resolved that any arms embargo imposed by the United States must apply to all the parties to a dispute, and not to the aggressor alone.

The Geneva Conference was not impressed by the American proposals. The renunciation of all offensive weapons proposed by Roosevelt might sound like a simple formula; but in practice, which weapons were offensive and which defensive? Had the Foreign Relations Committee supported Roosevelt by giving him power to identify an aggressor and stop arms shipments thereto, the French might have felt a certain reassurance and the Germans a certain impulse to caution. But by tying the Administration's hands, the Committee forbade American participation in a really solid system of collective security. All that remained was a rather vague scheme for a passive modification of American neutrality.

As the Disarmament Conference passed into a new deadlock, the fears of German withdrawal were translated into reality. Unquestionably, Hitler was encouraged by Japanese successes on the plains of Manchuria and in the hills of Jehol; undoubtedly, even moderate Germans were irritated by the French demands for special guarantees before they would grant the Reich equality in armaments. In June, the conference broke up to await a clearing of the political atmosphere. Mussolini had revived his plan for a treaty of guarantees signed by Britain, France, Italy, and Germany, and some statesmen hoped that this might improve the situation. But during the summer the position deteriorated. Japan's angry withdrawal from the League, the failure of the World Economic Conference, the ending of war-debt payments amid American chagrin and bitterness, the fighting which had broken out between Bolivia and Paraguay over the Gran Chaco, the worsening of the world depression—these charged the air with defeatism. The Disarmament Conference was to reassemble at Geneva on October 16. Busy preliminary discussions took place among the Foreign Ministers, with Norman H. Davis participating. A proposal for a five- or eight-year period during which armaments would be gradually limited, while Germany moved by successive stages toward equality, seemed to be gaining favor.

Then on October 14, Hitler exploded a bombshell which blew the Conference sky high. He announced Germany's withdrawal from both the Disarmament Conference and the League. Defending his decision on the radio, he declared that Germany meant to pursue peace, but that the persistent refusal of other nations to recognize the material and moral equality of the Reich had made the step necessary to vindicate her dignity. Consul-General Messersmith next month informed the State Department that while Germany would constantly profess a desire for peaceful cooperation, she would "fight shy of all conferences" on disarmament and collective security, and would continue rearming with might and main. All prospect of further progress by the Disarmament Conference was at an end.

Seeing the hope of disarmament lost in political animosities, the United States in November, 1933, quietly withdrew its delegate from the Conference. Norman Davis explained that America was willing to assist in reducing armaments, but was resolved to stand aloof from the complications of

European politics. He sailed for home on November 4. Most observers thought that his departure wore an air of finality, and the German press blazed with such headlines as "America's Knockout Blow to the League of Nations."

One gain was made during the year. On November 17, 1933, President Roosevelt announced the resumption of diplomatic relations between the United States and the Soviet Union. This action, accomplished by an exchange of letters, was generally approved even by those who condemned the tyranny and the secret police system of Russia, for it seemed anomalous to refuse recognition to a country which covered one-sixth of the world's land surface and counted 160 million people. Senator Borah, who detested Communism but had no fear of contact with it, and who gave so many Americans letters to Moscow officials that he was called "Russia's unofficial passport bureau," had long championed recognition. Sympathetic articles on Russia had appeared in 1929–33; cordial books had been written; and many manufacturers and merchants found the prospect of increased Russian trade alluring.

The terms of settlement represented a difficult negotiation. Certain claims had to be left for future adjudication and, though Washington expected Russia to settle its old debts, Moscow later boggled over the inclusion of any interest, finally paying nothing at all. The Soviet Government waived all demands for damages from the American Siberian expedition in the World War. As for Communist propaganda, the Soviet Government made sweeping promises. It engaged not only to refrain from any Governmental act which would injure the prosperity or security of the United States, but also to give no harborage to any organization which aimed at the overthrow by force of the political or social order in America. This promise was violated, and in 1935 the United States had to protest against a Comintern meeting in Moscow which laid plans to promote Communism in the United States. Nor did Secretary Hull's hopes for large expansion of Russo-American trade find realization, for in commercial matters Moscow (failing to get a loan from the newly created Export-Import Bank) remained suspicious.

Only in the political and moral spheres did recognition represent a marked advance. The handclasp with Russia, which joined the League in 1934, did something to emphasize the isolation of Germany and Japan, while intercourse with Soviet citizens became easier. Russia was aloof and half-hostile still, but the atmosphere had improved.

Early in 1934 another liberal policy of the Administration won a victory in the passage of Hull's Trade Agreements Act. Authorizing the President for three years to negotiate agreements with other countries by which, in return for trade concessions, rates of the Smoot-Hawley Tariff might be reduced as much as 50 per cent, it opened the way for a revival of foreign commerce. As Roosevelt pointed out, the volume of American exports had dropped in 1933 to less than half of the 1929 level. Hull's influence in Congress proved invaluable in rolling up large majorities for the bill, which passed the House 274 to 111, and the Senate 57 to 33. When Roosevelt signed it on June 12, a new era in American tariff history opened; for the law was renewed again, again, and yet again.

In general, however, 1933 closed and 1934 opened not merely in gloom, but amid apprehensions of trouble and conflict far greater than any known since Versailles. In the Far East the League had suffered humiliation and discredit—and the United States had lost prestige. In Europe efforts to substitute an improved system of collective security for the armed ascendancy of France and the Little Entente had failed, and that ascendancy had suddenly become precarious. The American Government, its first hopes of a quick economic recovery disappointed as autumn brought a slump, was preoccupied with home problems. Two powers, Japan and Germany, had defied the moral sentiment of the world, and chosen paths that led into —what? Nobody knew, but men began to fear the worst.

CHAPTER II

On two fronts of foreign policy, and only two, was the Roosevelt Administration able to make substantial progress in the years 1933–34. One was in the restoration of diplomatic relations with Russia; the other was in the enlargement of friendly intercourse with Latin America. Nothing except Anglo-American cooperation was nearer to Secretary Hull's heart than the cultivation of mutual confidence among the twenty-odd nations of the New World.

When the Administration took power, economic depression blackened the skies of all the Latin-American republics. At the nation's very doors Cuba was sunk in misery, its discontented population clamoring for an end of the hateful Machado regime. Farther south, one revolution had followed another. Beginning with a revolt in Santo Domingo in February, 1930, uprisings had taken place in Bolivia, Peru, Argentina, Brazil, and Guatemala during that year, and in Panama, Chile, Ecuador, and Salvador during 1931. The depositions of Hipolito Irigoyen in Argentina and President Carlos Ibanez in Chile were especially dramatic. American assistance was plainly desirable. In his inaugural address, Roosevelt declared: "In the field of world policy, I would dedicate this nation to the policy of the good neighbor." Hull believed that the principles he wished to advance in the Old World could have little power unless they first bore harvest in the New. Fine words alone would have counted for little with the Latin Americans. The radical aims, humane spirit, and economic liberalism of the New Deal, however, soon earned the admiration of such progressive nations as Mexico, Brazil, Chile, and Uruguay. The vibrant personality of Roosevelt, the patent honesty and elevation of Hull, equally won their liking.

It was plain that the new Administration meant to reinterpret the Monroe Doctrine, that it would warn all aggressors, particularly Japan and Germany, from the New World, and that it would lower tariffs to stimulate trade. Hull said again and again that he meant to give rigorous adherence to the principle of non-intervention. No other meddling would be attempted. Before long the common American front was being strengthened.

The Cuban problem was adroitly solved without intervention. Impoverished by the fall in sugar prices, the island was on the verge of revolt. The brilliant Sumner Welles, a service man of fine edu-

cation and ability, had been appointed Assistant
Secretary of State in charge of Latin-American
affairs. On April 21, 1933, he was transferred to
Havana as Ambassador, with power to negotiate a
treaty giving Cuba a quota-market for sugar in
return for concessions to American exports. With
Roosevelt's approval, he undertook to mediate the
dispute between Cuban factions. The Administration made it plain that it would welcome the withdrawal of Machado, and when Cuban troops revolted, that tyrant hurriedly left the country.

His successor, Dr. Carlos de Cespedes, proved
unable to control the situation, and Welles proposed "a strictly limited intervention" in his behalf, with the landing of forces at Havana and
other ports. This Hull refused to countenance; and
when a bloodless revolution installed Ramon Grau
San Martin in the Presidential palace, the United
States made no move to interfere. Instead, when
San Martin was shortly followed by Carlos Mendieta, Roosevelt on the advice of the new Ambassador, Jefferson Caffery, and of Hull, informed
representatives of seventeen Latin-American nations that the United States would recognize the
new regime; thus demonstrating his readiness to
accept any *de facto* government. He believed that,
as he had recently said, it was only when political
disturbances within an American country affected
other nations that they became matters of con-

cern, and that then they were "the joint concern of a whole continent in which we are neighbors."

Having thus emphatically repudiated intervention, the Roosevelt Administration removed a long-standing grievance by abrogating the Platt Amendment of 1901. This had restricted Cuba's power to negotiate treaties or incur debts, had given the United States the right of intervention to suppress acute disorder, and had authorized the acquisition of lands for American naval stations. Sumner Welles drafted a new treaty which discarded the whole arrangement (except that the Guantanamo base was retained), and it passed the Senate with but one negative vote. Congratulations came from various Latin-American nations.

The first clear evidence that the good neighbor policy would return golden dividends appeared at the Seventh Pan-American Conference in Montevideo in December, 1933. Depression was weighing down the whole globe, the London Economic Conference had just failed, and the Disarmament Conference seemed on the point of collapsing at Geneva. But despite the continuance of the Chaco War between Bolivia and Paraguay, the Montevideo meeting was a brilliant success. Twenty nations attended; ten, including the United States, sent their Foreign Ministers. It was the first time that an American Secretary of State had gone to such a gathering. As soon as the delegates measured

Hull's mind and character, they showed a remarkable willingness to trust him. When the question of intervention was brought forward, an elaborate convention for defining the rights and duties of states was submitted. It contained the following clauses:

ARTICLE 8. No state has the right to intervene in the internal or external affairs of another.

ARTICLE 11. The contracting states definitely establish as the rule of their conduct the precise obligation not to recognize territorial acquisitions or special advantages which have been obtained by force, whether this consists in the employment of arms, in threatening diplomatic representations, or in any other effective coercive measure. The territory of a state is inviolable and may not be the object of military occupation nor of other measures of force imposed . . . for any motive whatever even temporarily.

Hull cordially subscribed to this, asking only that the terms of Article 8 be defined. He felt safe in saying that "no government need fear any intervention on the part of the United States under the Roosevelt Administration."

The Montevideo Conference adopted no fewer than 114 recommendations for the promotion of inter-American amity. A resolution for the reduction of trade barriers by reciprocity treaties, with the maintenance of the most-favored-nation clause in all tariff arrangements, was particularly noteworthy. Equally important was a resolution calling upon all the nations to sign five pending peace treaties, including the Kellogg-Briand Pact. Repeated efforts were made to bring Paraguay and Bolivia to terms, with the result that a temporary truce was signed. Altogether, Hull was justified in saying that the meeting "thoroughly demonstrated the success of international conference as a method of settling important questions and advancing the general welfare." Roosevelt firmly supported his stand in disclaiming any wish to keep intervention alive.

Montevideo proved a great landmark in the history of Pan-American relations; moving forward from it, Hull later wrote, "We were able to develop a marvelous structure of friendly and trusting cooperation." Other steps soon followed. In his message to Congress at the beginning of 1936, Roosevelt declared that the good neighbor policy was "a fact, active, present, pertinent, and effective." The decisions taken in Cuba, Haiti, and Central America had proved that this was true.

The gloomy year 1936—the year of the Italo-Ethiopian War, Hitler's reoccupation of the Rhineland, and continued Japanese aggression on the mainland of China—witnessed widespread disorders in Latin America. Though fighting in the Chaco was stopped by a protocol signed on Janu-

ary 21, 1936, the boundary dispute there remained unsettled. Revolutions occurred in Paraguay and Bolivia; strikes attended by violence
broke out in Argentina and Chile. In Venezuela,
the death of the loathsome tyrant Juan Vicente
Gomez precipitated civil disturbances. Fortunately,
none of the disorders was really serious, and the
termination of the Chaco warfare seemed to offer
an opportunity for strengthening the peace machinery of the Hemisphere. At Montevideo some
important principles had been laid down. Since the
next Pan-American Conference would not occur
until 1938, and since the world scene was so stormy,
should not a special meeting be held to arrange a
common front in the event of any crisis?

Roosevelt and Hull, thinking so, on January 30,
1936, invited all the Latin-American states to send
delegates to Buenos Aires to consider how they
could strengthen the fabric of peace. Perhaps,
Roosevelt wrote, it could best be done by ratifying,
with amendments, all the inter-American peace
instruments already negotiated; perhaps by the
creation of new instruments of peace. In any event,
he would not displace the League, but supplement
and reinforce it. Acceptances were received, and
after ten months of hard preparatory work by the
State Department, on December 1 (just after
Japan and Germany concluded their Anti-Comintern Pact), the Inter-American Conference for the

Maintenance of Peace opened in Buenos Aires. Hull headed a delegation which included Sumner Welles and A. A. Berle, Jr. President Roosevelt, just reelected, voyaged to the gathering in the cruiser *Indianapolis*. As he stepped ashore in Argentina to receive the most enthusiastic ovation which that country had ever given any visitor, it was evident that the gathering would be of world-wide importance.

The purpose of Secretary Hull, who became the leading figure of the conference as soon as Roosevelt returned home, was to perfect the solidarity of the twenty-two Pan-American nations on a practical program of peace maintenance. In a notable address on December 2 he described the "Eight Pillars of Peace," which included education against war, frequent conferences, support of the Kellogg Pact, and the adoption of liberal commercial policies. He had to take due note of the fears of many delegates that the creation of a stronger Pan-American fabric would lessen the power and prestige of the League. Dr. Saavedra Lamas of Argentina, President of the gathering, who had just been given the Nobel Prize for his work in halting the Chaco War, felt strongly on this point, and so did others. They stubbornly opposed Hull's proposal for the creation of a permanent Inter-American Consultative Committee and for a common neutrality policy if any war began in the

Americas. Compromise was necessary; and out of animated discussions finally emerged two conventions and a protocol, surmounted by a general Declaration of Solidarity.

One convention dealt with collective security. The nations signing it agreed that if hostilities in any part of the world should present a threat to their peace, they would consult together on co-operative action. No commitment as to the character of this action was involved. Whether the undertaking would have any more practical efficacy than the paper agreement of the Kellogg Pact remained to be seen.

The second convention dealt with neutrality. Signatory states engaged to meet the provisions of five existing peace treaties, and also agreed that, if war broke out between any of them, they would all meet to consult upon a common neutral policy for preventing its spread. They might or might not resort to embargoes on war materials and war loans, after the fashion which had now been set by the United States; and they were all free to adjust their policy to their own laws and to other treaty obligations, including the League Covenant.

The supplementary Protocol of Non-Intervention went well beyond the limits fixed at Montevideo. Any intervention by one nation in the affairs of another was defined as a matter of concern to all, and was described as a threat to peace, justifying a resort to the consultations provided for in the Convention for Collective Security. In signing this Protocol, the United States took a long step toward satisfying her apprehensive Latin-American neighbors.

The Declaration of Solidarity was simply a comprehensive statement of general principles. It reaffirmed the Stimson Doctrine by declaring that the forcible acquisition of territory was not to be recognized. It condemned any intervention in the affairs of another state, or any attempt to collect money claims by force. Every dispute in the American family was declared subject to settlement by arbitration, conciliation, or adjudication. Though general in terms, this Declaration really did do something to strengthen the existing peace agreements.

About the two Conventions, the Protocol, and the Declaration of Solidarity were clustered a variety of lesser instruments. A panel of jurists was set up from which, in the event of threatened hostilities, a group of mediators could be selected. Permanent commissions were created to study plans for the prevention of disputes and to help give effect to existing agreements for the elimination of their causes. Resolutions were passed declaring for equality of treatment in international trade, and for the gradual lowering of tariffs by bilateral agreements. Not least important, a number of projects for intellectual cooperation were voted. Indeed, the conference touched on nearly every phase of Pan-American activity. Its concrete agreements, which were promptly ratified by the Senate, were important, and still more important was the atmosphere of general good will which it generated—an atmosphere for which no one deserved more credit than Cordell Hull. "The very fact of the conference itself," he said on December 23, "should offer to other quarters of the world an impressive demonstration of the value of concert and cooperation."

All in all, by the end of 1936 a new era had opened in the relations of the United States and its sister republics. Intervention in the Caribbean had ended, most Americans hoped forever. Even in Cuba, so close to American shores and so important to the American economy, the quadruple revolution (Machado to Cespedes to Grau San Martin to Mendieta) had occurred without landing of American troops and with no application of pressure outside of normal diplomatic channels. Through reciprocal trade treaties, as authorized by legislation of 1934, Secretary Hull was doing his utmost to assist the badly strained economies of the Latin republics. The treaty with Cuba in 1934, for example, did much to halt the fall in Cuban-American trade and put needed dollars in the pockets of ragged Cuban peasants.

With Mexico, the relations of the Roosevelt Administration were cordial in the extreme. A claims settlement to cover damages to American property during the revolutionary period was signed in 1934. When the Mexican Government in 1936 took drastic action against all foreign owners of oil properties, ordering the expropriation of their holdings, Hull contented himself with mild expostulations and a request that the subject be submitted to arbitration. Josephus Daniels made a signally popular Ambassador in Mexico City.

The problem of relations with Canada was unique in character and pleasantly easy. The white English-speaking populations of the Dominion and the United States were practically indistinguishable. They were governed under the same political principles, listened to the same radio programs, read the same books, and thought the same thoughts. Outside Quebec, most Canadian labor unions were part and parcel of the American Federation of Labor or (after 1936) of the C.I.O. The largest American and Canadian corporations operated with little care whether their customers and stockholders lived under the Union Jack or the Stars and Stripes. No boundary in the world was so nearly invisible. In short, the two lands had a cultural, social, and moral unity which made the thought of bad relations between them an absurdity. To Hull as to his predecessors, harmony with Great Britain and the Dominion was the main cornerstone of American foreign policy.

It was obvious in 1933–36 that the New Deal was having a profound effect upon Canada. The National Recovery Act, with its industrial codes and more liberal provisions for labor, compelled the Ottawa Government to adopt certain responsive measures and raised some Canadian prices. Prohibition repeal opened a market for the Canadian liquor industry so carefully kept alive throughout the "dry" era. The devaluation of the dollar lent an immediate and tremendous stimulus to the gold-mining industry of the Dominion. Altogether, the partial recovery of the United States gave the Canadians certain substantial practical benefits, and threw some rays of sunshine into the Canadian scene. A smaller "New Deal" was even attempted by Prime Minister Bennett.

Roosevelt took a warm interest in the project for deepening the St. Lawrence Waterway—a scheme for admitting ocean vessels to the Great Lakes while developing new sources of hydroelectric energy—and pressed earnestly for Senate ratification of the treaty signed in July, 1932. Opposition by Atlantic seaports proved too strong. In trying to improve trade relations, Secretary Hull was more successful. The two Governments in 1935 reached an agreement for reciprocal tariff reduction, and in 1938 it was greatly enlarged.

This second treaty was the result of triangular negotiations among America, Canada, and Britain, and in fact the American-British agreement was signed the same day. Both Roosevelt and Hull found the Canadian Prime Minister, Mackenzie King, a congenial spirit, and frequently expressed their regard for him and for the Dominion. The President made a particularly memorable statement when in 1938, during the Czechoslovakian crisis, he opened an international bridge across the St. Lawrence. Speaking at Kingston on August 18, he said: "The Dominion of Canada is part of the sisterhood of the British Empire. I give to you assurance that the people of the United States will not stand idly by if domination of Canadian soil is threatened by any other empire." This statement, which he personally inserted in a speech written for him by the State Department, was cordially appreciated both in London and Ottawa.

Though the Dominion had a population of but eleven millions, its agricultural and industrial strength made it an important power. "When I went to Canada," Hull has written, "I had the feeling that I was visiting home folks." It cannot be too often repeated that, in facing a troubled and in part hostile world, the American Government could take great satisfaction in the warm friendship of the entire British Commonwealth of Nations, and of almost the entire Latin-American family.

CHAPTER III

A NEW moroseness of outlook in foreign affairs possessed many Americans after the Japanese conquest of Manchuria, Hitler's rise to power, and the debt cancellations. Since the Old World was ridden by devils, they would have done with it. This pessimistic belief in withdrawal was rooted partly in the despair of the economic depression, partly in pacifism, partly in the contrast between the bright aspirations of 1918 and the dark political realities of 1933, and partly in a guilt complex arising from the consciousness of duties unperformed. It had three main effects. First, it brought about a reinterpretation of history to justify American abstentions, "proving" that other nations had always been bad beyond redemption. Second, it led many isolationists to attempt to destroy all distinctions between nations democratic and totalitarian, peace-loving and aggressive, painting them in nearly the same hues. Finally, it prescribed a future policy of narrow self-regard. Innumerable Americans felt that internationalism, defined as half foreign machinations, half credulous idealism, had brought about America's participation in the First World War, and this had in turn given birth to the depression. Secession from Europe, political, industrial, cultural, was an old American tradition; the time had come for new and final secessions.

The most irrational result of this cynicism was a tendency to view all foreign powers with the same hostility. The war-debts question afforded a pertinent example. All defaulting debtors were lumped together, although Great Britain, with which the sharpest bargain had been driven, had paid far more than any other. Later a still more striking example was furnished by the neutrality legislation. It was so cast as expressly to forbid executive discrimination between aggressor states and victim states. A good many who voted for this procrustean legislation frankly asserted that all Old World nations alike were steeped in sin and violence.

The fact was that the restless forces of upheaval active in the world filled conservative Americans with uneasiness and suspicion. Through the windows of the press, the radio, and the lecture platform, they looked upon a turbulent and threatening scene. Fascist Italy, struggling against the serpents of poverty, ignorance, and tyranny like a Laocoön; Nazi Germany, self-tormented, at grips with economic forces it could not master, and lashing out blindly in its desperation; Russia a Sisyphus striving to meet ever-elusive "goals"; Poland, Hungary, Yugoslavia, all filled with unrest; Bolivia mobilizing her entire manpower to attack the Paraguayans; India racked with political discontent and religious antagonisms; China still chaotic and torn by factional war; Africa awakening from her ancient apathy. It was too complex to understand, too overwhelming to offer a challenge to American helpfulness. The best course seemed simply to turn a shrugging back upon it. It was easier to try to shut it all out; to turn to the comfortable theory that the United States might live to itself alone.

The first clear token of the new temper was the passage of the Johnson Act in April, 1934. Senator Hiram Johnson, whose hatred of alien forces matched his boundless ignorance of them, and whose old-time progressivism made him especially antagonistic to international finance, prepared a bill to punish by heavy fine or imprisonment the purchase or sale of all bonds issued by foreign governments defaulting on their war debts. Hundreds of millions of these securities were held by American citizens. To strike at delinquent governments, Senator Johnson was willing to cause these citizens heavy loss. The Senate Judiciary Committee reported the bill favorably, but State Department objections helped block its passage. It was then amended to eliminate from its operation existing loans and to apply only to future issues, which it forbade.

The bill was an exhibition of spleen, designed not to protect American investors but to injure foreign nations. It offered an impediment to world recovery, for it blocked the extension of credits on which a revival of world trade might partly depend. Nevertheless, it passed both houses with little opposition, and despite the grave objections stated by the Treasury and State Departments, was signed by President Roosevelt. Its chief immediate effect was to deprive the United States of the ten-million-dollar token payments which Britain would have maintained; for such "tokens" did not save her from the stigma of default.

In the large view, the war debts were inevitably suspended by the world-wide depression; a depression for which the United States bore its share of responsibility. The American Government had taken special measures to suspend or reduce many forms of debt at home (mortgages were a conspicuous example) and to give debtors a variety of indulgences. An American President had acted to suspend German reparations for one year. Not only Britain but Italy and Czechoslovakia were now prepared to maintain the token payments, but after the Johnson Act these countries declined payment because, as Czechoslovakia put it, the remittance had lost its "symbolic and practical meaning." Inevitably, the law deepened the general ill-feeling at home resulting from the debt-service suspension. Abroad, it naturally accentuated the hostility to "Uncle Shylock," for both willing and unwilling defaulters resented the insult. Only a few sensible voices were raised. A number of American journals copied the statement of the London *Economist* that whereas the British annuity paid in 1923 was equivalent to six months' exports from Britain to America at that period, the annuity due in 1932 represented four years' exports at the later rate.

When Great Britain ceased payments, it was with an explanation which deserved wider attention than it got. Downing Street, in a note to the State Department, set forth that Britain had paid $2,205,000,000 out of a total original debt of $4,277,000,000; that other nations had paid only $679,000,000 out of a total of $4,714,000,000; that after lending $7,800,000,000 during the war to its Allies, the British Government had paid the United States not only everything it had received in return, but nearly as much again from its own treasury; that Britain's wartime Allies had now ceased all payments to her, thus greatly worsening her financial position; that transfers of any large sum to America would disarrange the world's exchange system; and that the Johnson Act gave the British an alternative of paying everything or nothing. While this last statement was not strictly true, it had much force. As payments ceased, American sentiment in general simply dismissed all debtor states in the same terms—welchers, cheats, fair-weather friends. Finland was covered with praise for maintaining payments, less because she deserved eulogy—her debt was trifling, and she alone among debtor states had a large favorable trade balance with America—than because this was a means of reproaching Britain, France, Italy, and the rest.

Another token of the rising tide of isolationism lay in the fresh rejection of the World Court idea at the beginning of 1935. That the Court had done excellent work nobody could doubt. Every President from Harding to Roosevelt had desired American entry. When Congress in June, 1935, passed a joint resolution approving American membership in the International Labor Organization, many people hoped that the door to the Court was at last swinging ajar. The I.L.O., to be sure, was not only completely independent of League management, but was operative in a field which had almost no political implications—a field, too, which engaged the close interest of American labor leaders. But popular distrust of the Court had been founded mainly on sheer prejudice, and prejudice always yields in time to reason. The arguments that the Court was a tool of the League, that it might injure vital American interests, that it would strike down the Monroe Doctrine and meddle with domestic issues like the tariff and immigration, that entry would be a long step toward back-door admission to the League, and so on, were sheer nonsense. Surely, hopeful men said, obstructionists could now be pushed out of the way.

We have good reason for believing that a decided majority of Americans emphatically wished entry. Both party platforms in 1932 had called for it. A heavy majority of newspapers, led by the New York *Times* and *Herald Tribune*, and a long list of church bodies, women's organizations, labor groups, peace societies, and other agencies, still demanded action. The thinnest of barriers seemed to separate the Senate, which adopted a resolution for affiliation with five reservations, and the Court members, who had boggled at one of these five. A committee of jurists, with Elihu Root its leading spirit, had tried to break down this barrier. Root prepared a protocol for American accession which embodied compromises apparently satisfactory to the Court, to the State Department, and to two successive Presidents, Hoover and

Roosevelt. Secretary Hull was anxious for action, and urged the President to move. On January 5, 1935, two days after the new Congress opened, Roosevelt called Senate leaders into conference with State Department officials to take up the question of immediate adoption. On January 9, 1935, the Foreign Relations Committee favorably reported the resolution.

But it was a delusion to think that ratification would be easy. Key Pittman and other Democratic Senators were lukewarm. Once more the bitter-end isolationists rallied all their strength. The World Court had become a symbol. In itself, membership would have been innocuous even from the Borah-LaFollette standpoint; but it would have raised a banner of triumph over the internationalist breastworks, and filled the isolationist camp with dejection.

As both sides closed in for the final fray, bitter passions were aroused. The Hearst press rallied the ignorant masses of the large cities against the Court, appealing especially to Irish-Americans and German-Americans. A demagogic Catholic priest of Detroit, Charles E. Coughlin, kept the radio singing with his phobias. A mushroom organization, well financed, sprang into activity overnight to defeat the Court. Every type of exaggeration and misrepresentation was used. The freedom of America, screamed isolationist editorials, broadcasts, magazine articles, and speeches, was at stake. Millions were urged to write or wire, and in the brief Washington debate some 200,000 telegrams were delivered to Senators and Representatives.

The opponents of the Court had three great advantages. First, they could employ appeals to the basic emotions of fear, anti-foreign prejudice, and dislike of risk, while their opponents had to appeal to reason. Second, the fact that America had gotten along fairly well outside the Court appeared to outweigh the vague and dubious advantages of joining it. But above all, the depression seemed to offer good reason for concentrating all the nation's energies on the home front, while the dangerous turmoil in Europe furnished still better reason for keeping aloof from all commitments and complications.

In the Senate vote taken January 29, adherence was defeated by 36 Noes to 52 Ayes, seven more votes being needed to make up the necessary two-thirds. It was a victory for apprehension, rancor, and ignorance, and a sharp defeat for the Administration. At a critical hour in world history, it weakened the arm of the American Government and the voice of democracy and peace.

The role of the President in all this was interesting. He and Hull had been primarily responsible not only for the general liberalization of foreign policy during 1933, but for a whole series of praiseworthy innovations. The recognition of Soviet Russia; the quiet enlargement of American co-operation with the League; the final surrender of the old doctrine of intervention in Latin-American relations; the proposal at the Disarmament Conference to give at least passive assistance to collective measures against an aggressor power; the first steps in a world-wide program for lowering tariff barriers—these constituted a remarkable record. But in the critical period of the Senate debate, January 26–29, Roosevelt failed to intervene. He had consistently avoided any acts so abrupt as to alarm public sentiment or estrange those Progressives who wished to combine reform in home affairs with isolationism in foreign policy. Hiram Johnson, Burton K. Wheeler, Robert M. LaFollette, Jr., George Norris, David I. Walsh of Massachusetts, and a long list of others were ready to aid the New Deal but would balk if asked to assist an international program. Roosevelt needed their help in his domestic program and in the 1936 campaign. Hence his refusal to put the full weight of his influence behind the Court.

One force behind the growing swell of isolationist opinion was the revisionist impulse in dealing with the history of the First World War. This rewriting of wartime history had been begun in isolationist appeals of 1918–20. John Kenneth Turner (whose book *Shall It Be Again?* went through three print-

ings in 1922), Hartley Grattan, and others carried
it forward. Woodrow Wilson appeared in these
publications not as hero but dupe. Now suddenly
this interpretation swelled to the proportions of a
cult, taking special hold on old-time isolationists,
Republican haters of the Wilson tradition, enemies
of Britain or France, people who had long secretly
or openly favored Germany as against the Allies,
disillusioned and grudge-nursing groups, and that
part of the rising generation which prided itself on
ultra-realistic and cynical views of the past.

After the close of the war Sir Charles Oman in
England, Pierre Renouvin in France, and other
scholars had used the war documents published by
Germany (*Die Grösse Politik*) and other powers
in making a revisionist study of the origins of the
European conflict in 1914, which interlocked effectively with the restudy of American action in 1917.
Sidney B. Fay brought out in 1928 two amply
documented volumes on the *Origins of the World
War* which showed that the guilt of Germany had
been exaggerated, and that of Austria, France, and
Russia underestimated. His conclusions were
shortly amplified by the more moderate and judicious work of Bernadotte Schmitt, *The Coming of
the War* (1930), which although friendlier to the
Allies did a good deal to lighten the record of the
German Empire. Walter Millis's *Road to War*, cir-
culated widely in 1935 by a book club, combined

cool research, incisive analysis, and sardonic style
in a fiercely hostile scrutiny of the Wilsonian record
of 1914–17, oversimplifying a highly complicated
period of history. Scholars read these works; magazine and newspaper writers popularized their ideas;
and they gradually colored much of American
thinking. Meanwhile, pacifist ideas affected the pulpit, the daily and monthly press, and even the
movies; "The Big Parade," a film by Lawrence
Stallings released in 1933, was anti-war in tone.

This new spirit of mingled cynicism and idealism
(for most pacifists were idealists), of revisionism
and progressivism, found lodgment in school and
college faculties, and laid a heavy imprint on the
minds of American youth. All intellectuals studied
and not a few accepted the idea of national self-
containment. Lawrence Dennis, Wallace B. Don-
ham, and Charles A. Beard all published works
urging the abandonment of international ideals and
the adoption of narrowly nationalist policies. Fic-
tion, emphasizing the price youth paid in the hor-
rors of war, strengthened the revolt against international responsibilities. A long list of novels and
plays dealt with war as needless and revolting, and
some explicitly treated American participation in
1914–18 as a criminal abandonment of the country's true interests. John Dos Passos, Ernest Hem-
ingway, Upton Sinclair, and numerous less famous
men laid hold of the emotions of the reading pub-

lic. As the Hearst press appealed to the ill-informed masses of twenty cities, and the Chicago *Tribune* sowed seeds of anti-foreign feeling throughout the Middle West, other journals catered especially to the radical-minded. The *New Republic* and *Nation* both held up all foreign activities in the most critical light, frequently assailed American participation in international activities of a political nature, and harped on the necessity for complete detachment from all forces that would lead to a new World War. Some of both the best and the worst impulses of American opinion mingled in the new abstentionist movement.

In vain did such public men as Newton D. Baker, in *Why We Went to War*, and such scholars as Charles Seymour present a balanced (though necessarily incomplete) history of events, demonstrating that the mainspring of American participation had been a worthy desire to uphold what most authorities considered old principles of neutral rights, a shrewd regard for the nation's safety, and a just resentment of German injuries that had become intolerable. Many Americans wanted to believe the new thesis. It excused so many prejudices, and supplied so many reasons for the popular policy of continued abstention!

As early as March, 1914, Philip Snowden had delivered in the House of Commons a rasping indictment of the "armament ring," an international group which he declared responsible for constant war scares created in order to raise the defense expenditures of various governments into bloated figures. Krupp, Nobel, Vickers, and Bethlehem Steel had been arraigned again and again as fomenters of international disturbances. Something had been said, even while the First World War was still raging, of the fact that the French failed to bomb the Briey basin, which in German hands was a source of death to *poilus*, but whose steel works the French expected to recover. Indeed, Socialists, pacifists, and journalists had often exposed the unquestioned fact that munitions interests constituted a powerful international web, that they had a business motive for keeping nations fearful of each other, and that they used strong pressure on premiers and parliaments. The League Covenant had referred to the admitted evils of the manufacture of arms.

In 1929 a curious incident led to a revival of old suspicions. William B. Shearer, a former employee of the Navy Department who had been hired in 1927 by American warship builders to attend the Geneva Naval Conference, and whose publicity work had aroused hostile comment there, sued his employers for $255,655 which he alleged they still owed him. This became a public scandal. President Hoover asked for a Congressional investigation. The fact that during the conference Shearer had fed the jingoist, anti-Japanese, anti-British, big-navy section of the American press with figures and figments, that he had tried to influence American naval officers in Geneva against limitation, and that in every way he had exerted himself to block agreements, was quickly recalled. The head of the British delegation, Lord Bridgman, had protested to the chief American delegate at the time. When the investigation took place, important shipbuilding executives, including Charles W. Schwab and Eugene Grace of the Bethlehem interests, Clinton L. Bardo of the New York Shipbuilding Company, and Frederick P. Palen of the Newport News Company, explained that they had not known what Shearer was really doing, that they had been victimized by his irresponsible activities, and that they really wanted world peace—though they also wanted dividends. But it was shown that Shearer had been their highly paid lobbyist, that he had boasted of his influence over the American press, and that he had done much to earn the article which a Geneva paper ran about him: "The Man Who Wrecked the Conference."

Suspicion was general that corporations which manufactured or exported munitions had long fomented wars. This suspicion was exploited by pacifist and isolationist groups to make the public believe that it had been victimized by such profiteering elements in 1917 and might be betrayed again.

The House Committee on Foreign Affairs early in 1933 held hearings on the shipment of arms and munitions. Three representatives, at least two of whom later discredited themselves by highly injudicious acts, held a colloquy full of absurd misstatements:

MR. MELVIN J. MAAS: Do you believe that traffic in munitions is in itself a cause for war?

MISS JEANETTE RANKIN: Yes; I believe that wars in the past have been started in that way.

MR. MAAS: . . . It appears that the real causes of war are economic.

MISS RANKIN: Yes.

MR. HAMILTON FISH: We forget the fact that we entered into the war because we insisted on shipping munitions of war, and Germany, not agreeing to our plan of shipping munitions, attacked our ships on the high seas and forced us into the war, as I remember it.

MISS RANKIN: They did not force us. We got in. Of course, we could have stayed out. . . .

MR. MAAS: We started shipping munitions to the Allies because we had loaned them money, and the reason for lending them money was so that they could buy war supplies in this country, which was an economic cause and not a militaristic cause.

At this inquiry the airplane manufacturers and the arms manufacturers gave evidence that a considerable part of their business lay in foreign shipments, the proportion varying from 10 per cent in some small-arms concerns to a high percentage in the aircraft industry. They contended that the export of arms and munitions in volume was important to national preparedness for war. It was easy to accuse them of acting on the principle that their prosperity depended upon the existence of fear and friction in other parts of the globe.

Thus a growing volume of newspaper and magazine articles was devoted to exposure of the munitions industry and its alleged machinations. Senator Gerald P. Nye, a leading isolationist, introduced a resolution for a special Senate investigation. It was adopted April 12, 1934. As soon as the resolution passed, Vice-President Garner made the blunder of appointing Nye himself, instead of some judicious representative of the Democratic majority, as head of the investigating committee. Secretary Hull believed that a worse choice could not have been made. Amid a clamor for taking the profits out of war, the inquiry began on September 4, 1934, with public hearings. For nearly ten years, the United States had failed to ratify the Geneva Convention for the suppression of the international traffic in arms, though urged to action by President Hoover and Roosevelt. Now it hastily did so—with a crippling reservation.

The inquiry might have been one of the healthiest undertakings of the time. Properly conducted, in the quiet, efficient way in which a similar investigation was held in Britain by a Royal Commission, it would have been exceedingly valuable. As it was, a sharp distinction must be drawn between the actual evidence upon the munitions trade, and the deductions drawn therefrom by Nye and other isolationists.

The evidence itself contained much that was sensational and shocking. It was proved that armament firms of different nations were closely related in various ways, exchanging information, partitioning business, and even sharing patents; that they hired lobbyists and agents who conducted intrigues of an E. Phillips Oppenheim luxuriance; and that they paid "commissions" in government circles which amounted to bribes. It was shown that in some instances (fortunately few) American army and navy men had acted to promote the trade of American munitions firms. It was shown also that various Government departments in Washington, anxious to keep the armament industry vigorous enough to furnish weapons in a defense emergency, had lent their good offices in promoting sales to foreign nations. Great disgust was aroused by the revelation that during the war the companies building ships for the Government had made profits ranging up to 90 per cent; that after obtaining cost-plus contracts, they had added questionable charges; that they had obtained changes in contract dates in order to avoid war taxes; that they had paid huge bonuses to officers, and concealed profits as rentals; that they had bought Government-built yards at preposterously cheap rates; and that in general, they had profiteered mercilessly. The Nye investigation as resumed December 4, 1934, showed that nearly all American munitions manufacturers had been helping rearm Germany, despite the Versailles Treaty; that the Remington Company had been certain in 1933 that "nothing will be done to interfere with business" in Bolivia and Paraguay; and that the DuPonts and others had easily evaded Government controls over munitions exports.

On December 12, 1934, President Roosevelt took a hand by suddenly announcing that measures should be drawn "to take profits out of war," and appointing Bernard Baruch and Hugh S. Johnson heads of a committee to lay plans. He simply revived an old idea, propounded by earlier Presidents and supported by the American Legion. Socialist doctrines on war had found wide acceptance, influencing newspapers and textbooks. Baruch had assisted a special commission, appointed under Congressional resolution in 1931, to explore means of equalizing the burden of war and removing the profit motive from it, a commission whose ultimate report placed emphasis on the mobilization of manpower and industries. Nye took a suspicious attitude toward the President's proposal. He thought it might be an effort to forestall his own report by a Baruch-Johnson plan which would be more acceptable to the War and Navy Departments and the munitions industry. "Our hearings," he said, "have revealed that departments of the government are co-defendants with the munitions industry and the profiteers." These departments, therefore, ought not to write remedial legislation. Congress in due course set up certain controls for the manufacture of munitions, and forbade arms exports except under licenses issued by an Arms Control Board consisting of four Cabinet officers, with the State Department in administrative charge.

Unhappily, Nye, besides recklessly exploiting the investigation for personal publicity, permitting witnesses to make such false accusations against foreign statesmen that Britain, Mexico, China, and other governments protested, and in general, thinking more of headlines than facts, used the investigation to buttress his tendentious view of American entry into the First World War. He, with La Follette and Hiram Johnson, had long asserted that the United States was forced into the conflict by bankers, arms-makers, and other profiteers. Here was an opportunity to strengthen the charge, to attack the Wilson Administration for political reasons, and to cater to hyphenate voters. The committee majority impugned Wilson's integrity; it smeared the Allies with filthy innuendo. Nye began

making speeches in which he twisted the evidence
to support his general thesis. When the time came
for the final report, he inserted a long memorandum
which placed the blame for the bad relations of Germany and the United States during 1914–17, not
upon the Imperial German Government which had
ordered unrestricted submarine warfare, but upon
the American Administration which had maintained the historic principles of the freedom of the
seas and the right of a neutral to trade with belligerents. This legitimate trade, declared Nye's memorandum, was in "materials for murder"; insistence
on maintaining freedom of trade demonstrated
"America's complete lack of neutrality"; and when
Germany turned to ruthless submarine warfare,
this was because Wilson's course compelled it "inevitably."

Altogether, the exaggerations and distortions of
the Nye Committee had a sinister influence, especially in areas where the isolationist press gave it
a sounding board. Only specialists had time to
examine the multivolumed record of hearings, and
few were those who read even the 1,400 pages of
the final report. But the juicy bits of testimony, the
headlines, the startling deductions of committee
members, and the lurid reports of Washington correspondents were read with avidity. A general impression was diffused that if J. P. Morgan, the
Bethlehem Company, and other bankers and muni-

tions makers were not responsible for the war of 1917, they had much to do with it; and that if profits were drained out of war, peace would be fairly well insured. Another idea was also forced into the American mind: the belief that Congress could be better trusted to keep the peace than the Executive, and that the President should be placed under tight rein in the field of foreign policy. Such simplifications were highly attractive to countless citizens.

They were obviously too simple, and Congress balked at the more extreme legislation proposed. In the spring of 1935, the House did pass the McSwain Bill providing that immediately upon the declaration of war the President might freeze prices, license all manufacturers, dealers, and public services except newspaper and magazine publishing, and "commandeer" the material and financial resources necessary to the prosecution of the war. Also, upon the declaration of war, a tax of 100 per cent upon all excess war profits would go into effect. Baruch opposed the tax, saying that it would remove all incentive to effort and cripple the war production, and he was backed by Hugh S. Johnson and others. Though Nye and Vandenberg in the Senate held out for the levy, it did not become law. Such confiscation might hamper the nation in some dire exigency. Meanwhile, a number of measures upon neutrality were also introduced in Congress. Among them were resolutions by Nye and Bennett Champ Clark, which, to the consternation of Roosevelt and Hull, were reported out of Key Pittman's Foreign Relations Committee in June. The Administration was anxious to kill them. But they helped show that the general impact of the Nye investigation upon public sentiment was tremendous.

It was an impact the greater because it coincided with a sudden shift in the foundations of the American attitude toward foreign policy. In the first years of the depression the country had wavered. It was interested primarily in economic recovery. If an international policy would promote recovery, then such a policy should be followed. The Hull trade treaties, the good neighbor policy toward Latin America, the warmer features of the hot-and-cold Roosevelt policy toward Europe, found favor largely because they seemed likely to promote prosperity. But after the rise of Hitler and the Japanese onslaught upon China, the American people turned toward a new objective: peace. Their one desire was to avoid that impending war which H. G. Wells, in a prophetic utterance of 1933, predicted would begin by 1940. Americans began to think about international problems in place of domestic problems, but to think of them in terms of avoidance of conflict. Another great world war might ruin civilization, and the United States was determined to keep aloof.

This was the temper of the nation as Mussolini set about his preparations for the conquest of Ethiopia, and as Hitler pushed his rearming to the point of absolute defiance of the Allies. It was Mussolini who first copied the Japanese example in the use of brute aggression. Needing the resources of Ethiopia, he had long fixed covetous eyes on the one last unappropriated bit of Africa. In December, 1934, a border clash of Italian and Ethiopian forces at Walwal gave him the pretext he wanted. The Emperor Haile Selassie offered to arbitrate; Mussolini declined, insisting upon reparations; and the League took up the issue. It was evident that the Italian dictator intended a complete conquest of Ethiopia, and that nothing but war or economic sanctions amounting to war could stop him.

Into the tangled, dreary, abortive story of the efforts of undetermined statesmen to halt this arrogant leader we need not go. The central difficulty lay in the growing Nazi threat. Already Germany was so strong that she might fly at the throats of other powers before they knew it—or so they feared. It seemed imperative to maintain a united front on the part of Britain, France, and Italy against the Nazis, or at least to do nothing which would force Italy into Germany's circle of satellites, which already included Austria and Hungary. Hitler, as his associates have since testified, now dominated every situation in Germany. From 1933 on-

ward he made every important decision, and set
the timing for every new step. While somewhat
deferential toward his first Foreign Minister, the
veteran diplomatist Constantin von Neurath, he
was autocratic in his control of lesser figures in the
foreign sphere. He thought always in military, not
political, terms, and disliked any process of bargaining and compromise; either he must give way,
or his opponents must yield. Never having been
outside the German lands, never having read foreign literature, he found the psychology of other
peoples, and particularly of the British, difficult to
comprehend.

At the beginning of 1935 the French Foreign
Minister, Laval, had concluded an agreement with
Mussolini which provided for the settlement of all
pending differences and for consultation if Germany made any aggressive moves. It is probable
that Laval secretly made promises of French com-
plaisance regarding Ethiopia; at any rate, he had
no mind to see the hard-won entente with Italy disturbed. Nor had Britain—nervous over her Mediterranean communications, and her fleet weaker in
fact than on paper—any desire to run risks. Her
Foreign Secretary, Samuel Hoare, was a cautious,
peace-loving man. Both the British and French
Foreign Offices, as the Hoare-Laval Plan presently
showed, would have been willing to compromise
the difficulty by giving Italy part of Ethiopia and a

special economic status in the region, compensating the Abyssinians elsewhere. But Mussolini would have no compromise.

The most tragic feature of the whole affair was not that Italy completed her bloody conquest and took over the administration of a semi-barbarous state. It was that in their indecisive maneuverings the British and French Governments failed either to vindicate their view of international ethics or to retain Mussolini's friendship, while their backing and filling at Geneva humiliated the League and proved that weak nations could place no dependence upon it. If the Anglo-French leaders had taken a determined stand upon principle, cutting off all Mussolini's oil supplies, and, if necessary, blockading Italy in the hope that the ensuing hostilities would be brief, they would have broken the triple Western alignment, but might have reaped a great and permanent reward in return. If, on the contrary, the British and French had abandoned principle, declared that Italy under the existing circumstances must have her way, and insisted upon firm pledges from Mussolini in return, they could later have partially justified their course by considerations of *haute politique*. As it was, their halfway sanctions, cutting off a long list of commodities but not disturbing the one essential item of oil, estranged Mussolini but did not stop him. The Duce denounced his former Allies and turned to-

ward Hitler. As for the League, these partial sanctions proved that its guarantees to small member-
nations were worthless unless the great powers
underwrote them with genuine energy.

But if Anglo-French policy failed to show either
wisdom or principle, the conduct of Congress also
left much to be desired. Its isolationist and pacifist groups now felt more suspicious than ever that
the Old World powers were intent mainly on defending their empires; and these groups were determined to pass neutrality legislation which would
leave the President no discretion. Against the warm
protests of Secretary Hull, who had been working
on a very different kind of law, Key Pittman took
his stand with the extremists. Late in August, 1935,
Congress passed the Pittman resolution providing
for a mandatory embargo upon implements of
war, to be applied by the President to both belligerents. It also authorized the President to declare
that American citizens traveling on ships of a belligerent nation did so at their own peril. Roosevelt
reluctantly accepted the legislation and imposed
the arms embargo on both Italy and Ethiopia just
before the League Council met to take steps. During October, when the League voted partial sanctions against Italy, when Britain sent some of her
largest ships into the Mediterranean, and when
Mussolini concentrated 50,000 crack troops in
Libya to menace the Suez Canal, a number of dis-

tinguished Americans were urging cooperation with the League. In opposition to them, two of the country's principal pacifist organizations, the Conference on the Cause and Cure of War and the National Council for Prevention of War, were vocal for neutrality, the latter calling for an embargo not only on arms, but on loans, credits, and raw materials useful in war. Father Coughlin's Union for Social Justice was active on the same side.

The League, its principal nations anxious to maintain peace, placed no embargo upon oil or other absolutely vital materials for war. American exports to Italian Africa swelled from an average of $25,000 a month during 1934 to nearly $600,000 during November, 1935. Large shipments from Germany also reached Italy. Secretary Hull on November 15 issued a statement calling for a moral embargo, saying that although shipments of oil, copper, scrap, and motor vehicles were not illegal, they were contrary to the Government's policy. Had the League, under Anglo-French leadership, shown sufficient courage to halt all exports of oil, the United States would probably have taken decisive steps to that end. But it must be considered that Britain and France would have met the brunt of the ensuing attack; the United States, three thousand miles away, had nothing to fear.

Long before Mussolini had completed his hazardous operation, Hitler had seized the golden opportunity which it gave him. The Reich officially admitted early in 1935 that it possessed a good air force. On March 16, Hitler announced that the Versailles Treaty limitations on military strength were dead, declared that his new army would be over 500,000 in strength instead of 100,000, and introduced conscription. A conference of Britain, France, and Italy was hurriedly held at Stresa, where some agreements and resolutions were drawn up—but no positive action was taken. This "Stresa Front" quickly crumbled under the impact of the Ethiopian quarrel. The strength of the French alliances in eastern Europe, meanwhile, appeared less formidable than before; for with great skill, Hitler during 1934 had concluded a ten-year non-aggression pact with Pilsudski, the Polish dictator.

One token of Germany's rising power was the announcement in June, 1935, of a naval agreement between the Reich and Britain. German ingenuity had made the "pocket battleships," limited by the Versailles Treaty to 10,000 tons, marvels of compact power. It was now impossible to prevent the Reich from building as heavily as it pleased; and the British therefore saw many advantages in a treaty under which Germany promised to build surface ships only to 35 per cent of Britain's tonnage, and submarines only to parity. Taken in itself, the agreement had much to commend it.

But it gave serious offense to France, which had not been consulted.

During the first four months of 1936 one sensational event after another registered the triumph of force and brutality in various quarters of the globe. In Tokyo murder had now become a political commonplace. But even Tokyo was shocked to its center by the "incident of February 26," when on a chilly morning, the ground deep with snow, about 1,500 heavily armed soldiers made simultaneous attacks upon a number of the principal leaders of the Empire. Such distinguished figures as Prime Minister Okada, Viscount Saito, Prince Saionji (last of the Genro or elder statesman), and Korekiyo Takahashi, the distinguished public financier, were marked for assassination. Four high officials, including two Cabinet Ministers, were cut down in cold blood. Admiral Suzuki was seriously wounded. The War Office, police headquarters, and other Government buildings were seized. Fortunately, large forces remained loyal, warships were brought into Tokyo Bay, martial law was proclaimed throughout the disorderly area, and after three days the revolt was suppressed.

The incident pointed to a smoldering discontent. Japan had profited little from her Manchurian adventure, and had lost much. Throughout China and the wide regions of the South Pacific where Chinese did business, the anti-Japanese boycott had been fanned into full flame; and Japanese steamship lines, factories, banks, merchants, brokers, had all felt the blow to their activities. Japan had been forced, soon after the beginning of hostilities in 1931, to drop the gold standard, and the yen had fallen to about two-fifths of its former gold value. This meant a heavy added burden to the Japanese people in paying for imports and meeting debt requirements. Exports, on the other hand, had been stimulated, but at the cost of world-wide complaints that Japan was "dumping" her goods. Japan's credit in the sphere of international finance had fallen, and though she had never defaulted on a foreign obligation, her bonds were selling at heavily depreciated rates. While her war industries were booming, the rest of the Japanese economy was seriously injured. The budget was a constant worry, the weight of taxes was crushing, and the discontent of the agrarian masses was acute. On the profit side of the ledger, the Japanese had gained the right to own and lease land in Manchuria; but no large-scale migration to Manchuria had taken place, primarily because the Japanese with their relatively high standard of life could not compete with the Chinese of low standards. Manchurian minerals were not of much immediate value, and they, like the market for manufactured goods, might have been gained without invasion and occupation.

Immediately after the Japanese murders, Germany made use of the opportunity which Italy's quarrel with Britain and France had given her. Sunday, March 7, 1936, saw 35,000 of Hitler's troops marching into the Rhineland, expressly demilitarized by the Versailles Treaty and the Locarno Pact. Calling together the representatives of Britain, France, Belgium, and Italy in Berlin, Hitler announced that his Government regarded the Locarno agreement as dead. Within three days the reoccupation of the Rhineland was complete. Hitler appealed to the German people for support, laying his case before a plebiscite which this same month gave endorsement by 98.7 per cent of a total of almost 45,000,000 votes cast. Inside Germany, in fact, the coup was greeted with tremendous jubilation, as the chief step toward restoring self-respect and securing the complete freedom of the German nation. In the shock tactics of the period, this was one of the greatest blows of all. It was a flat violation, as the League Council presently decided by unanimous vote, of both Versailles and Locarno. It went far toward rendering Germany's western borders impregnable, for by October the number of troops in the Rhineland had been doubled, and defensive works were well under way. The success had added immensely to the prestige of the Reich.

As German leaders had foreseen, hesitation was followed by acquiescence. France might have moved to eject the German troops had she been sure of united support. But opinion in France itself was divided. Belgium suggested delay and concilia- tion; Italy was flatly opposed to action—she still seemed on the verge of possible war with France and Britain; and the British, who simply would not go to war to prevent Germans from holding all Germany, declined to join in armed action. Those French Ministers who wished to put their columns in motion were overruled. To be sure, Russia, Czechoslovakia, and Yugoslavia offered support, but the Polish-German non-aggression pact stood in the way of quick movement, and Russia was but slowly regaining her strength. The decision of the League Council (March 19) that Germany had violated her engagements was not followed by sanctions. On May 7, instead, the French, British, and Belgian representatives attending the League Council decided to postpone any action with re- spect to German infraction of the Locarno Pact.

As Europe recovered from the first impact of this stroke, Mussolini completed his conquest of Ethi- opia. Defying the League, he thrust his mecha- nized armies forward over the central Ethiopian plateau, employing bombers and mustard gas with- out mercy upon the half-armed tribesmen. As April, 1936, closed, all organized resistance was ending, and Haile Selassie was about to flee from his domain. On May 5, Italian troops swept into

Addis Ababa in clouds of fire-streaked smoke, with
carnage in their rear. Another dictator was enjoying
his triumph. Rome, Berlin, and Tokyo could con-
gratulate one another, and make preparations for
further acts which, if not concerted, were at any
rate thoroughly harmonious.

During 1935, a secret German military mission
had arrived in Tokyo. The ostensible reason was
that the Germans wished to build an airplane car-
rier, lacked the technical knowledge, and could
more readily ask help from Japan than from the
English-speaking powers. The mission was given
the information it needed. Then toward the end of
1935 the subject of a political compact between
Germany and Japan was tentatively explored.
Both countries saw manifest advantages in the idea.
Since the Japanese invasion of Manchuria, the relations between Tokyo and Moscow had become
seriously strained; since Hitler's rise to power Germany had never been friendly to Russia, and the
two countries were now close to open enmity. A
treaty between Japan and Germany would do much
to keep Russia under restraint. Negotiations were
carried on in Berlin by the Buero Ribbentrop, quite
divorced from the Foreign Office, which knew
nothing of them. The principal German negotiator,
one Van Raumer, invented a name for the new
association, the "Anti-Comintern Pact." This was
better than "non-aggression pact," which hardly

fitted either the aims or the geographical situation of the two nations. In view of the fact that the Russian Government had disclaimed any association with or responsibility for the Comintern, the new treaty could be called "ideological" and defended against any Moscow criticism. The Anti-Comintern Pact was duly signed in the autumn of 1936.

Meanwhile, Japan had been making quiet arrangements to inspire a demand for autonomy by the five provinces of North China—that is, to detach these provinces from China proper. When Chinese leaders refused to carry out their instructions, stiffening their resistance, Japanese troops on November 27, 1935, began to move southward through the Great Wall. By early December they had occupied the railroad junctions at Peiping and Tientsin, and had deployed more than ten thousand troops in this area. Secretary Hull issued a statement on December 5 that the United States was "closely observing what is happening" in North China, and that same day Samuel Hoare, speaking in the Commons, warned Japan that her actions were arousing world suspicions at a most unpropitious moment. But for Tokyo it was propitious!

The tide of anti-war sentiment was now rising to full flood in the United States. All confidence in the collective-security system represented by the League was dying away. Of course, it could be argued that if the United States had been a member of the League, Geneva's action in Manchuria and Ethiopia might have been prompter, firmer, and more compelling; but most Americans did not think so. It was plain that, in a crisis threatening war, the League meant the three or four great powers which would bear the brunt of a conflict; that these powers were seldom if ever perfectly united and mutually faithful; and that the more a power loved peace, the more it was likely to flinch from the actual shock of conflict. When Japan threatened to fight any nation which intervened between her and her Manchurian prey, President Hoover declared he would never take the United States to war in such a cause. When Mussolini threatened to fight any nation that intervened between him and Ethiopia, the British Government resolved not to risk war. The graver kind of economic sanctions, it was also plain, were tantamount to war. A League which possessed such imperfect unity, which was bound to a procedure involving delays, and which had no police force, was helpless in facing a powerfully armed nation bent on aggression. Neville Chamberlain, speaking on June 10, 1936, told a British audience that "surely we must admit that we have tried to impose upon the League a task which was beyond its powers." He thought it might be possible to find "a more practical method of insuring peace by regional arrangements"—but at any rate, he was sure the League had failed.

International order had broken down. Americans saw that a new era of "international anarchy" had begun, and that it might well be a prelude to a second World War. Most Americans were determined to keep the republic out of it. Under the circumstances, it was hardly possible to realize that a bold restoration of collective security offered the only real safety. As the wave of a new isolationism and a new pacifism swept the country, Congress turned in a panicky rush toward legislative measures for keeping out. Imperfect neutrality had carried the United States into the First World War, men falsely reasoned; laws for double-riveted neutrality might keep it out of any second conflict.

CHAPTER IV

EXPERIMENTS IN NEUTRALITY

THE first busy year of Roosevelt's New Deal had hardly ended when, as we have indicated, a marked divergence became evident between the foreign outlook of the Administration and that of Congress. At first glance it may seem strange that a President so popular as Roosevelt, a Secretary of State so beloved as Hull, should be so little trusted in the conduct of European relations. Actually it was not strange at all. Roosevelt and Hull had different sources of information from those of Congress—as time proved, much superior sources; they saw the world picture in far broader perspective, with more detail and color; they had to look further ahead and estimate contingent disasters that Congress ignored; they thought of the national interest in an international setting, whereas most Congressmen thought of local interests in a national setting. The Administration was keenly alert to perilous trends that Congress hardly perceived.

Secretary Hull had before him such reports as

that which Douglas Miller, Acting Commercial Attaché in Berlin, made to the State Department on April 21, 1934. It was the determined purpose of the Nazis, reported Miller, to effect "the expansion of German territory and growth of the German race until it constitutes the largest and most powerful nation in the world, and ultimately, according to some Nazi leaders, until it dominates the entire globe." The German people, suffering from defeat and indignity, jealous of other lands, inflamed by reckless slogans, were uniting behind the Nazi gangsters who made them such extravagant promises. This union became more nearly perfect as the Nazis shut off all outside avenues of intelligence, and by use of press, radio, platform, schools, parades, and noisy meetings whipped up the masses to crusading frenzy. They talked of peace; but, wrote Miller, the firmer their control, "the more certain is a large-scale war in Europe some day." Their leaders were "narrow, ignorant, and unscrupulous adventurers," who meant to aggrandize themselves and Germany at the cost of France, Poland, Czechoslovakia, and any other nation they could bring within their power. Similar testimony came the same year from Consul Geist in Berlin. German youth, he reported, were systematically imbued with a fierce love of militarism, the glories of conquest being exalted without any attention to the restraining virtues of justice and mercy. It was difficult, he added, to see how this bellicose spirit could be restrained from bursting forth into aggressive war "toward the end of this present decade."

From observers in Japan gloomy reports and ominous predictions had now become commonplace. There, too, as Ambassador Grew had been writing since his arrival in 1932, the people were steadily being whipped into a war fever. They had been brought to believe the conquest of Manchuria a matter of such supreme national interest that nothing could have halted their armies except superior physical force. Everywhere Grew found a profound distrust of America and a sharp animosity toward American policy. The army was playing up the danger of future war with the United States in order to get larger appropriations. When Hull made a speech in 1935 which irritated the Japanese, the resultant outburst convinced Grew that the Japanese army chiefs were aping the German militarists of 1914. They were fast creating a dangerous national temper. Their formidable military machine, the Ambassador informed Hull, might easily break through all restraint at any time. Once Manchuria had been gained, Tokyo made efforts to allay the American hostility; but this phase (which coincided with threats by aggressive elements against the Dutch Indies) was to be short-lived.

It was possible for the diplomatic corps to give

confidential information on the rising menace of
Germany and Japan to the State Department,
which conveyed it to Roosevelt; it was not possible
for Roosevelt or Hull to share much of this information with Congress or the country. Most alarming
of all were various intimations that the aggressive
powers of the Orient and Occident seemed to be
reaching at least a vague understanding. In May,
1934, the American Military Attaché in Berlin reported evidence suggesting "the existence of un-
usually close and friendly relations between Germany and Japan even to the extent of a possible
secret alliance." Grew in Tokyo reported during
the next year indications of "an intimate exchange
of views and information going on between Japan
and Germany."

Roosevelt, with his special information, tended
to speak and act with a boldness which alarmed
isolationist Congressmen. Delivering an address in
Washington as 1933 closed, he declared that it was
not the peoples, but certain small groups of ambitious leaders, who wanted war—leaders who were
managing to mislead and pervert docile masses of
followers. Nine-tenths of the population of the
globe, in his opinion, wished for continued peace,
sought no territorial expansion, and were willing
to transfer expenditures from armaments to more
productive purposes. If the remaining tenth could
be permitted to do their own thinking, free from

control by duces, fuehrers, and warlords, the world
would be secure. Secretary Hull was still more out-
spoken. In May, 1934, he made a notable address
in Washington. Pointing to the rise of the dictatorships, the feverish rearmament of nations, and the
universal lapse into economic nationalism, he
charged Americans to be vigilant. Unless the unprecedented challenge of the time was met, the
would would be in danger of "another period of
long night—such as the Dark Ages." In Williams-
burg, Virginia, the next month he described the
international situation as offering ground for the
"gravest apprehension." But neither President nor
Secretary could specifically refer to the information
that reached them from Embassies abroad. Their
utterances therefore struck pacifists, appeasers,
and isolationists as an unnecessary and dangerous
provocation of Germany and Japan.

Nor did the Administration fail to match its
warning words with measures of preparation. The
State Department anticipated late in 1934, while
Japan was blocking progress at the London Naval
Conference, that Tokyo would shortly give notice
that she would terminate her obligations under the
Washington Naval Treaty. The very day (December 29) that the notice was handed Hull by Ambassador Saito, the Navy Department told the
press that the 1935 naval maneuvers would be
held west of Hawaii. At once Western Senators as-

sailed the move, the radical weeklies inveighed against it, and important church bodies projected a movement to have it canceled. In Japan the warlike element seized upon the announcement as justification for their high military and naval demands. The most expert observer of the Japanese situation, however, was emphatically in favor of the Pacific maneuvers. When the president of the Federal Council of Churches called on Ambassador Grew on April 1, 1935, to ask his advice, Grew told him that cancellation would give Japan the impression that pacifist elements were so powerful in America that any country could ride roughshod over rightful American interests; it would heighten Japanese arrogance, and it would hold the door open to more aggressive tactics. The maneuvers were duly carried out.

The aspect of foreign policy on which the Administration and Congress came nearest seeing eye to eye was in making ample provision for national defense. Douglas MacArthur, the Chief of Staff, presented forcible pleas in his annual reports of 1933 and 1934 for army expansion. The War Department appropriation in the spring of 1935 authorized an augmentation of the army from 115,-000 enlisted men to 165,000, while provision was made for more airplanes, motorized vehicles, artillery, and tanks. From the beginning of his Administration, Roosevelt took the keenest interest in improving the strength of the navy. One of the striking acts of his first year was his allocation of $238,000,000 under the National Industrial Recovery Act for building and equipping thirty-two naval vessels. Under the Hoover Administration the United States had followed the policy of disarmament by example, letting its navy sink much below the tonnage permitted by treaty. At the beginning of 1935 about one-quarter of its paper strength was past the technical age limit, as against about one-sixth for Britain and Japan. Secretary of the Navy Swanson had announced just after Roosevelt took office that the fleet would be built up to full treaty strength. This program was embodied in the Vinson Act, effective in the spring of 1934; a law which, appropriating no funds but laying down a detailed schedule, called for attainment of full treaty strength by 1942 at a cost of from $750,000,000 to $1,000,000,000. Unquestionably, public sentiment was behind this increase in armaments. Nor did it fail to elicit the fervent approval of Great Britain and the Dominions—particularly Canada and Australasia.

In nearly every field Roosevelt, despite his marked popularity, had constantly to bend an uneasy eye upon Congress. That body never ceased to display a tendency toward selfish and bumptious nationalism. In dealing with the tariff, large groups among the Democrats as well as Republicans constantly hankered after the fleshpots of protectionism. Secretary Hull's reciprocal trade treaties legislation was effective only for three years unless renewed; he and the President succeeded in getting the renewal in 1937, in 1940, and in 1943—but they always had to fight hard for it. As the State Department negotiated one trade agreement after another until a score had been signed, the liberal press applauded, and large areas of international trade profited. The two compacts with Canada and the arrangement concluded in 1938 with Great Britain were especially valuable. It could be said that the program merely modified the tariff wall instead of breaching it, but even a modification was important. Many Congressmen, however, viewed the victories of Hull in a grudging and carping spirit, while others were steadily obstructive.

The same nationalism, streaked with purely regional selfishness, appeared in the silver legislation of Congress. The act passed in June, 1934, launched the Government upon a broad silver-purchasing program which in the end cost American taxpayers hundreds of millions, and seriously injured the economies of other countries. The law, declaring it the national policy to maintain one-fourth of the monetary stocks of the United States in silver, directed the Treasury to purchase the metal at a price not exceeding fifty cents an ounce—this price later being raised. China felt serious effects from this legislation within two months. Her silver flowed outward, deflation began, prices fell, and the foreign-trade balance dropped. In vain did the Chinese Government protest to Washington; Hull had to reply that the policy was statutory and mandatory. Late in 1935 China, after much hardship, abandoned the silver standard. Mexico was plunged into similar difficulties, and in the end had to demonetize her silver coinage, and resort to a managed currency. In lesser degree nations all over the world suffered from the rise in silver, but the tyranny of the bloc of Senators and Representatives from the mountain states was never relaxed. In order to give a large domestic subsidy to special silver interests, Congress disrupted the financial mechanisms of friendly nations.

In treating with Latin America, and in interpreting the lessons of the good neighbor policy, Congress by no means saw eye to eye with the Administration. An interesting illustration of its attitude was presented in reference to Panama. That small nation occupied a hopelessly anomalous position. Through its middle, a cincture cutting it in two, ran the Canal Zone, leased by the United States in perpetuity and rigidly controlled by American agencies, though still under Panama's sovereignty. The original treaty of 1903 had granted the United States broad privileges in maintaining order, supervising the sanitation of Colon and

Panama, and expropriating lands outside the Canal Zone. As Panama developed strength and dignity, such restrictions aroused irritation. Year by year the old treaty grew more obsolete. Roosevelt and Hull took a liberal view, and soon after they entered office a new compact, which went to a remarkable extreme to conciliate the people of Panama, was written.

Under this treaty the United States surrendered its right to intervention to restore order; it gave up the power of expropriating land outside the Zone; and dropped its unilateral guarantee of Panama's independence. In the defense of the Canal it accepted Panama as equal partner. The original treaty had provided that the $250,000 annual rental of the Zone be paid in gold coin, and Panama had bitterly complained when she was recompensed in paper dollars worth only sixty cents in gold. Accepting her view, Washington raised the rental to $430,000. Still other provisions were designed to protect Panama merchants, who complained of excessive sales in Canal commissaries, and Panama workmen, who grumbled that the American authorities discriminated against them by hiring outside laborers. Altogether, the Roosevelt Administration dealt handsomely with a nation whose wishes it might easily have continued to ignore. For years the very word Panama had been a source of irritation to much of Latin America, and the grievances of the Panamanians had given rise to reproach in parliaments and press throughout South America. Now this blotch was sponged from the record.

Congress, however, did not accept the treaty without demur. Apprehension of Japan and her new navy was rising, and with it a conviction that the Panama Canal must be carefully safeguarded. The Senate Foreign Relations Committee held secret hearings. Some leaders hesitated to sanction all the proposed changes; they feared that a fascist government might arise in Panama and cooperate with Japan. Could the United States take any risks respecting the most vital link in its naval communications? A long delay ensued. In the end, the two governments exchanged notes by which Panama agreed that the United States might hold military maneuvers on ground near the Canal, and that if a sudden crisis arose, it might take instant measures to maintain the safety of the Zone. Thus reassuringly interpreted, the treaty was ratified. Final action did not take place until 1939, just before the world storm burst, but general faith in the outcome had produced a due effect in large areas of Latin America.

In the eyes of isolationists, the growing concord between the United States and Latin America pointed to the possibility of "hemispheric" aloofness from the Old World. The twenty-one republics

and the Dominion of Canada possessed every re-
source to make them impregnable and prosperous.
They might well set up their own system, leaving
Europe to welter in its hatreds; they could be safe,
happy, and free if they merely turned their backs on
the rest of the world. A few years were to prove
this view as foolish as it was selfish; to prove that
Latin America responded quickly to Old World
ideologies, that much of it was highly vulnerable,
and that the ocean was a path for conquest rather
than a barrier. But the doctrine for the time being
found wide acceptance. The view of Roosevelt and
Hull was necessarily more realistic. They knew how
indissoluble were the bonds, political, economic,
and cultural, between the Old World and the New;
they understood the perils which hung over the
Western Hemisphere. They held that the growing
cordiality of Latin America and the British Commonwealth toward the United States made a bold
international policy possible. Assisted by such
friends, America ought to be defending the interests of world democracy more trenchantly; the
Hemisphere should not be a fortress but a base.

Such was the situation when the general breakdown of the main safeguards of world peace, the
wave of pacifist and isolationist feeling in the
United States, and the public condemnation of
munitions makers following the Nye investigation,
combined in 1935–37 to produce an almost panicky

demand for legislation to keep America neutral in the next conflict. It was a portentous phenomenon, this demand for statute-book entrenchments of peace. If we forgot the perilous world situation, it would appear like other sudden crazes which have swept the country: the imperialist craze, the prohibition craze, and the anti-Red craze which followed the First World War. Overriding all reasoned objections, it found expression in legislation so crude and sweeping that the task of rational enforcement would have been difficult even under the best of circumstances. In the situation which actually developed, with great aggressor states attacking one weaker nation after another, it encouraged the masters of brute force by drawing a ring within which they could move without fear of even indirect American interference. In short, it was a disaster to the world.

This movement, which caught the Administration off balance, was not quite as sudden as it seemed. Its origins went back to the proposals for American consultation and cooperation with other powers in the event of a violation of the Kellogg Pact made under Hoover at the Geneva Conference on Arms Limitation in the spring of 1933, and to President Roosevelt's request that same spring for legislation empowering him to apply an arms embargo to any aggressor nation. Both the old Republican and new Democratic Administrations wished this discriminatory embargo power. Various writers assailed the suggestion as dangerous. A conference held by the Council on Foreign Relations in New York disclosed a sharp division of opinion.

Indeed, general agreement by the spring of 1934 that the old concepts of neutrality were out of date was accompanied by complete disagreement as to the type of revision needed. One school held with Stimson, Roosevelt, and Hull that the League, the Kellogg-Briand Pact, and the facts of current history made it imperative for the United States to advance further in what they saw as the eternal battle between right and wrong. It could not be neutral as between assailant and assailed. The opposite school held that moralistic policies were untenable, that the United States should not take sides, and that strict non-intercourse with all warring powers was the only safe path. By an early date in 1935 nearly twenty bills to keep the country out of war had appeared in Congress, and they represented a wide variety of views.

The State Department had for some time been working on neutrality with a keen sense of the complexity of the subject, and of the importance of vesting a wide discretion in the Executive. It held with Stimson that the day had gone by when a great nation like America could exercise a strict neutrality toward aggressor and victim alike; that under the Kellogg-Briand Pact a conflict became

of concern to everybody, and the aggressor should
be penalized. A committee in the State Department studied the question, and by the spring of
1935 it had draft legislation in hand. As the Ethiopian conflict and the repercussions of the Nye cir-
cus became pronounced, Secretary Hull felt greatly
perturbed. He told a press conference late in August that while it was important to keep the nation
from being drawn into hostilities, it was also important to do something to keep hostilities from
breaking out. If by passing hasty legislation the
country tied its own hands, making it impossible
for the Administration to use its influence against
an aggressor or to ship material aids to a victim of
aggression, then it put itself in a sad position.

Nevertheless, a majority of Congress and especially of the Senate subscribed to the hands-off-
completely doctrine. Their argument ran that in
the First World War the United States had shipped
munitions, it had lent money, it had permitted our
citizens to travel on passenger ships owned by belligerents, and involvement had come; *post hoc,
propter hoc.* If a second World War approached,
we should do none of these things. In the Chaco
War, Congress had given the President power
(1934) to stop arms shipments to both belligerents,
attacker and attacked, and he had used this power.
Now similar legislation should be applied to other
parts of the world. This hands-off-completely school

in fact contained many who thought all foreign nations wicked and predatory, and who were as quick to denounce the British democracy as the Nazi tyranny. In the controversy two different psychological attitudes were involved. One school regarded the arms embargo as a device for weakening the will to fight on the part of foreign nations; the other as a device for weakening the war pressure from munition interests and bankers at home. As long as the first view prevailed, much could obviously be said for discriminating between attacker and attacked, as Hull and Roosevelt desired. If the second view were taken, the more complete the stoppage of the arms traffic the better. After the munitions inquiry, a host of Americans accepted the second view without any special reflection. Such isolationist Senators as Nye, Bennett Champ Clark, and Hiram Johnson at once espoused it.

Hence it was that, as in 1935 Mussolini's demands on Ethiopia made a new war absolutely certain and threatened to involve half of Europe, a fierce insistence on rigid legislation now gripped Congress. The State Department fought valiantly to the end for a discretionary law, and was supported by Roosevelt and various Cabinet members. But the so-called neutrality bloc seized control of the situation; and with the aid of Chairman Pittman of the Senate Foreign Relations Committee, it presented an iron front against Roosevelt's demands for flexible legislation. Some Senators asserted in mid-August that they would use what Nye called "drastic means" to force action before adjournment. A flood of telegrams, letters, editorials, and resolutions at once descended upon Congress. Thus threatening a filibuster, the isolationist bloc forced Secretary Hull and the President to give way. As we have seen, the Pittman resolution, admittedly a mere stopgap to meet the imminent danger of an Italo–Ethiopian war which might involve various European nations, and to some extent a compromise between Senate and House, passed both chambers by almost unanimous vote, and with Hull reluctantly advising consent, was approved by Roosevelt on August 31, 1935. Stopgap though it was, it set such an unhappy precedent that Roosevelt later rued bitterly his failure to veto it.

The joint resolution sometimes called the Neutrality Act of 1935 was valid (so far as its mandatory features went) for only six months, or until February 29, 1936, for it was expected that more permanent legislation would soon be passed. It bore clear marks of haste. It provided that when or after war began between two or more foreign states the President should proclaim the fact, and it should thereafter be illegal to "export arms, ammunition, or implements of war" from the United

States to any belligerent, or to any neutral for transshipment to a belligerent. The National Munitions Control Board was set up to register persons engaged in the munitions business and issued licenses for shipments. No American ship might, under severe penalties, carry unlicensed cargoes of arms or munitions. The President could forbid submarines to enter American ports, and also had discretionary power to forbid American citizens to travel on ships of a belligerent country.

When Roosevelt signed the resolution, he voiced his reluctance and his belief that further study was needed. No branch of the Government, he pointed out, could foresee all possible future situations. Conditions might arise in which the "wholly inflexible provisions" of the new law would drag America into war instead of keeping it out. The Government ought to avoid entanglements, but it ought also to "cooperate with other similarly minded governments to promote peace."

When open warfare began between Italy and Ethiopia in October, the law received its first test. Roosevelt, as we have seen, immediately put the arms embargo into effect, and in addition proclaimed that American citizens would travel on belligerent vessels at their own risk. The Government refused to approve credits by the Export-Import Bank for shipments to Italy. Indeed, Roosevelt went further; using his executive powers in an area beyond the new law, he warned shippers that they would trade with the belligerents at their own peril, without diplomatic protection. Both Hull and the President were anxious to discourage all traffic with the warring countries, and issued a warning that "transactions of any character" with them would be without Governmental protection. We have noted the "moral embargo" which the State Department imposed on November 15 against shipments of oil, copper, scrap iron, and motor vehicles. Obviously, as Abyssinia had no ports, this was an embargo against Italy, and Roosevelt and Hull meant it to hamper that misguided country.

Instead of giving extended study to fresh neutrality legislation, as Roosevelt wished, Congress early in 1936 reenacted the existing law with few changes. An effort was made by the State Department, with the belated help of Senator Pittman, to improve the law by enlarging its scope and making Hull's "moral embargo" on abnormal shipments a definite feature. The new bill would have given the President power to hold to pre-war levels the exports to any belligerent of materials used in the manufacture of arms, ammunition, or implements of war, if he thought this would promote American security; or to refrain from such restrictions if he thought this would promote American security. The cooperationists supported the bill. They wished, indeed, to go further and allow the President to embargo shipments to an aggressor while sanctioning those to the victim. The isolationists, on the other hand, insisted that the nation stick to a cast-iron statute.

The cast-iron law, Walter Lippmann remarked, was equivalent to announcing: "I see two thugs about to start an assault on my honest neighbor next door. As he may expect me to hand him a stick to help beat them off, I am signaling the thugs to go ahead and I'll keep clear. I am neutral." Yet it prevailed. The opposition to all discretionary features was so pronounced that the State Department measure was cast aside and a more cautious bill was introduced in its stead. This merely extended the act of 1935 until May 1, 1937, with slight amendment of some of its terms, and with two new sections. One of them made the law inapplicable to any American republic engaged in war with a non-American power and not cooperating with a non-American state. The other and more important was directed against the bankers, forbidding them to lend money to a belligerent government, or to deal in any securities of such a government issued after the President's proclamation of a state of war. This short bill passed by heavy votes, with every evidence of public approval.

The United States was now thoroughly committed—in theory—to complete abstention from the supply of munitions or credit to any belligerent whatever. In theory, it was fully protected against espousing one side or another in a foreign war, against letting munition dealers or money lenders haul it toward the temple of Janus, and against what might be the excessive idealism of a Wilsonian type of President. In reality, the neutrality law had not operated as its authors intended in the European conflict, and it operated even more bunglingly in the new Spanish civil war. It had, in fact, no overt application to a civil war, which was a contingency that its authors had not foreseen or had not regarded as a possible cause of concern.

The so-called Spanish Civil War was really a prologue to the great conflict now approaching between the Axis powers and the Western democracies. As such, it aroused the most intense feeling in the United States. Only a small band of foresighted internationalists and a certain number of Negroes had been deeply stirred by the Ethiopian conquest; but tens of millions felt intensely over the Spanish carnage. The attempt to overthrow the Spanish republic, undertaken by reactionary militarists with the aid of considerable clerical groups, and abetted openly by Mussolini and Hitler, seemed to the majority of observant Americans a crime against freedom throughout the world. Ambassador Claude Bowers sympathized deeply with the republican regime. About three thousand Americans enlisted with the Spanish loyalist forces.

Millions of dollars were raised to buy them medical supplies, food, and clothing.

Although the neutrality law had no legal operation in this conflict, its moral effect was overmastering. In the past the United States and other nations had followed the policy of selling munitions to any established government striving to stamp out a revolt. During our own Civil War the North had obtained large shipments of war material from abroad; during the Calles–Huerta troubles in Mexico, Washington had permitted aid to go to Calles. But now Roosevelt and Hull, partly under the moral constraint of the neutrality legislation, partly because they wished to cooperate with the London Non-Intervention Committee, did all that they could to discourage shipments to either side in Spain. They invoked a moral embargo. Non-intervention, proposed by the French on August 1, 1936, and accepted in principle within a week by Britain, Germany, Russia, and Italy, was in its origins an honest attempt to limit a conflict whose ideological nature threatened to embroil all Europe. Unfortunately, it soon became clear that while the British and French fulfilled their engagements not to ship munitions or other aids, Italy, Germany, and Russia did not. Before long non-intervention degenerated into such a farce that it became somewhat difficult to justify the continued support of it by Britain and France. Their excuse was that it was more important to preserve the peace of Europe, and their own safety, than to prevent the over-throw of freedom in the Spanish Peninsula. Believing this correct, Roosevelt and Hull kept their policy in line with that of London and Paris even after the violations of the agreement by Italy and Germany became flagrant. Moreover, the President recommended a legal embargo against both sides to Congress, and on January 8, 1937, a Congressional interdict was duly applied.

In following this course, Roosevelt and Hull had the approval of all isolationists, all pacifists, and a great body of Catholics. They were contributing, they believed, to world peace. A very real fear of an explosion that might begin a new World War possessed Roosevelt, Stanley Baldwin, Neville Chamberlain (who became Prime Minister on May 28, 1937), Leon Blum, and Camille Chautemps—the leaders, that is of all the great Western democracies.

There was genuine ground for apprehending German aggression if Britain and France let themselves be tied down by conflict with Italy. It has since become evident that Hitler was watching eagerly for an opportunity to spring upon Czechoslovakia. The Fuehrer held a meeting on November 5, 1937, with his advisers, Von Neurath, Von Blomberg, Von Fritsch, Raeder, and Goering. He declared that conquest of Czechoslovakia and Austria was indis-

pensable, as a means of improving Germany's military position, to a great future thrust for the conquest of adequate living space. When should Austria be absorbed and the Czechs attacked? As soon
as France became immobilized by an internal crisis
or by war; and Hitler thought that a bloody conflict between Italy on one side, Britain and France
on the other, might take place in the summer of
1938 and offer a proper opportunity. He instructed
Von Fritsch to devote the winter to study of the
best means of breaking the Czech defensive ring of
fortifications and subjugating the little republic.

But the restriction of the conflict and the safety of
the Western democracies were purchased at a high
price. When the Fascist forces, which had undertaken the ruthless overthrow of the Basques in the
north, subjected undefended Guernica to a brutal
bombing attack, public opinion in the United States
was deeply moved. The "little world war" in Spain
dragged on until 1939. But long before that date it
was plain that Franco's nationalists would win the
cruel struggle, and make a deplorably tyrannical
use of their victory; it was plain that their triumph
would strengthen the Rome–Berlin Axis which was
formed in October, 1936. In this unfortunate development America's neutrality policy, no less than
the non-interventionist policy of Britain and
France, had played a distinct part; yet any alternative course might have proved more disastrous still.

In the spring of 1937 the American experiments with neutrality reached their unhappy climax. The old law was expiring and a new one had to be written. Once more contention grew bitter between those who believed the United States ought to help prevent wars and those who believed that it was sufficient for the country to keep rigidly aloof from them. Secretary Hull, with Roosevelt's support, waged an earnest fight for flexible legislation. Finding the Senate obdurate, the Administration tried to carry a sane bill through the House. There was no question now that a wide gulf separated the Axis aggressors from such victims as Ethiopia and Spain; that it was important to deter Hitler, Mussolini, and the Tokyo warlords. By the narrowest of margins the Administration bill was emasculated in the House. In the end the abstentionists once more carried rigid legislation; and this time it was so sweeping that the old American principle of freedom of the seas for neutral trade disappeared entirely. The fact was that Congress, facing the European confusion, had become more isolationist than ever.

In consequence of the Ethiopian and Spanish conflicts, men were anxious to extend the embargo system to certain raw materials vital to field operations. But talk of such action aroused the fears of cotton, oil, copper, and steel producers, and a special arrangement had to be hammered out with respect to their commodities. The most striking innovation of the new law was therefore its cash-and-carry provisions. Practically all the old neutrality stipulations were carried forward, and some were given greater stiffness than before. In addition, it became strictly unlawful to solicit or receive contributions for a belligerent; unlawful for an American citizen to travel on a belligerent ship; and unlawful to arm any American merchant vessel. These new features gave the law a triple-brass front that seemed to the Nyes, Wheelers, and Clarks to promise safety. But the really far-reaching additions were the cash-and-carry clauses on raw materials.

The new Act provided that not only arms, ammunition, and implements of war, but "certain articles and materials" as well should not be carried in American bottoms if the President thought an embargo necessary to the national welfare. The law did not define these materials, but in debate Congress made it clear that it expected all contraband commodities—oil, rubber, cotton, copper and other strategic metals, iron scrap, and so on—to fall under the ban. These goods might be sold to belligerents if they were paid for in cash, and if title passed before they left the United States. They might be carried abroad if the carrying were done by foreign vessels. Thus no American could lose if the goods were captured or destroyed. The Senate wished to make the cash-and-carry clauses mandatory; the House preferred to leave a certain latitude for the President in defining the list of commodities. He did not, of course, have any discretion whatever in favoring one belligerent against another—and this remained the fatal defect of the legislation.

While the law of 1937 was the high-water mark of the isolationist tide in the neutrality field, it was not passed without significant predictions that it might well prove futile. Some members of Congress lamented that it estopped the most powerful nation in the world from making any contribution to collective security. But it was really too late for such regrets; collective security had now irretrievably broken down. What was most memorable, in connection with the passage of the law, were the numerous assertions that it did not really fit the times, and would not long be effective. It had been modeled to suit the conditions which produced the First World War; but a quite new set of conditions was now producing the Second. Its proper title, said the New York *Herald Tribune*, was "An Act to Preserve the United States from Intervention in the War of 1914–18." Various members of Congress declared that circumstances might soon arise which would make mincemeat out of the act. Even Hiram Johnson, who spoke of it as a response to an emotional urge, predicted that it would not have continued efficacy.

Why did men make these prophetic utterances, which time was so fully to justify? Why did they not exhibit more faith in the Congressional handiwork? Because American anger, as it watched events in central Europe and in China, was slowly but steadily rising. The outrages committed by the Nazis and the Japanese, and the threat presented by the Rome–Berlin–Tokyo front, were causing innumerable plain citizens all over the land to wear a sterner mien. Moral neutrality was disappearing. It might be, reflective men were deciding, that this hideous enginery of aggression and cruelty would leave no safe room for neutrality—that neutrality would spell not safety, but dire peril.

CHAPTER V

THE NATION COMES TO ITS SENSES

THE great seal of the United States displays an eagle grasping an olive branch in one talon and a sheaf of arrows in another. Since the defeat of Woodrow Wilson the nation's policy in foreign affairs had been lacking in strong moral imperatives. The olive branch had been waved over Latin America, and had traced in swiftly obliterating sands the generalities of the Four-Power Treaty and the Kellogg-Briand Pact; but no policy had been enunciated for the defense of which the eagle would use her arrows. None had been defined because the majority of Americans assumed an attitude of moral lassitude in regard to world affairs. Perhaps some commanding political crusader might have shaken the people out of their apathy; but between 1920 and 1933 the United States produced no figure comparable with Thomas Masaryk, Jan Smuts, or Robert Cecil—leaders who believed in stating a noble world ideal and giving battle for it.

By sheer weight, this apathy remained dominant in the early years of the Roosevelt era. As the State Department later put it, "much of public opinion in this country did not accept the thesis that a European war could vitally affect the security of the United States, or that an attack on the United States was possible." It certainly did not accept the thesis that the welfare of other peoples was any vital concern of America so long as her own safety was assured. But in the middle thirties an awakening of public opinion began. We might term it the great rally, for it was a return to the idealism expressed under Theodore Roosevelt and Woodrow Wilson. Security and national interest were obviously involved. On one side it was a product of apprehension for the United States itself; the realization, in the State Department's words, "that the Axis design was a plan of world conquest in which the United States was intended to be a certain, though perhaps ultimate, victim." On a more impressive side it was produced by indignation over the bestialities of the Axis powers.

The growth of this militant new spirit would have been more rapid but for the unfortunate appeasement policy of France and Britain in 1936–38, and for the bloody purges in Russia. A series of unhappy developments within these three nations, in fact, weakened each and played into the hands of the Fascist states. The rise of the Front Populaire to power in France in June, 1936, under Leon Blum, was in its international bearings a clear misfortune. Blum was a man of keen intelligence and devoted patriotism; his party effected a number of long-needed economic and Governmental reforms; and he left the nation industrially stronger. But his Leftist groups inspired profound fear among the wealthy classes, and most capitalist leaders refused to cooperate with him. Internal divisions, soon to bring France to the very verge of ruin, became alarming. The republic seemed splitting into elements so antagonistic that civil war might soon result. In dealing with foreign issues, moreover, Blum was weakened by the fact that the Communist wing of his coalition was often bitterly opposed by the Socialist and Radical groups.

By comparison, Britain was a well-united nation, and the Conservatives supporting first Baldwin and then Neville Chamberlain were a coherent, harmonious party. But great excitement was aroused near the end of 1936 by the events which ended in the abdication of Edward VIII and the crowning of George VI. To other countries the crisis seemed to point to internal weakness.

In Russia, Soviet administrative terrorism had a long and gruesome history. All Americans knew the Cheka, organized in December, 1917, had slain tens of thousands during the civil wars of 1918–20. In 1922 it had been replaced by the OGPU, which in the ensuing years carried out countless executions. With uncontrolled power to arrest, banish, and execute, the OGPU kept Russians in a state of chronic fear. At first only small numbers were sent into exile, but after 1929 the deportation of "class enemies" assumed a mass scale. In 1932 a new Soviet law made it possible to punish by death any theft of state property; in 1934, any Soviet citizen who crossed the frontier without permission was made liable to the death penalty. What was more, dependent relatives of any fugitive from Russia were subject to deportation for five years into Siberia, without food cards. Russia was a prison house, much of it hidden behind what Winston Churchill later called the iron curtain; the state (as represented by favored groups) everything, and the individual nothing.

Against this background, the most dramatic series of trials in modern history was now to rivet the gaze of a horrified world. An alleged conspiracy to destroy the Stalinist Government had sprung up. In 1936 sixteen defendants, including such famous Communists as Kamenev and Zinoviev, had been put on trial, sentenced to death, and executed. Then in January, 1937, seventeen more defendants were arraigned, tried, and sentenced either to long prison terms or to death. Half a dozen were important political leaders; the others were engineers, bureaucrats, or careerists. The most prominent were Radek, long one of the foremost Communists; Pyatokov, credited with a leading role in the "success" of the great Five-Year Plans; and Sokolnikov, an able diplomatist who had become Assistant Commissar for Foreign Affairs. The word "trial" was a misnomer, for the defendants (after preliminary treatment) all pleaded guilty at the outset. Their prosecution was therefore not intended to secure conviction, but to furnish a dramatic spectacle for propagandist purposes. This propaganda, as Ambassador Joseph E. Davies recorded, was expected to serve three main purposes: to warn would-be conspirators of the dark fate which awaited them; to discredit Trotsky; and to whip up popular feeling against Germany and Japan.

The sensation aroused by the first trials was raised to new heights when in June, 1937, eight principal generals, including the famous Marshal Tukhachevsky, were also "purged." It gradually became known that throughout Russia trials of hundreds of thousands of defendants were taking place and that party purges were causing the sudden disappearance of immense numbers of leaders in politics, industry, agriculture, science, and the arts. Tukhachevsky was said to have admitted entering a German plot; others were accused of varied forms of disloyalty, ranging from minor sabotage to foul conspiracy. An atmosphere of terror enveloped all Russia. Precisely why these wholesale executions were carried out, precisely what actual guilt existed, and precisely what relations the purges bore to Russia's foreign policies, is not yet known. The *full* truth, since witnesses and documents have disappeared, will never be known. Some believed that an actual pro-German conspiracy had become widely ramified; others that Stalin was conducting secret negotiations in 1936–37 with Hitler, and when he had made sure of the latter's peaceful intentions, seized the opportunity to "liquidate" all his opponents, rivals, and ill-wishers.

What is certain is that Soviet unity and strength were heavily shaken, and Russian prestige fell to a sad level. Ambassador Davies was in London when news came of the killing of the eight generals. Returning to Moscow, he wrote Sumner Welles of what he had observed in western Europe. "There are many indications that France has lost faith in the power of her Russian ally," he commented. "I was impressed in England by the general feeling there that England would be in a sad state if she had to rely on France with her internal weakness and on Russia under the present conditions." His own view was that Russia was neither so weak as she was then supposed to be, nor so strong as the French and British had thought her three months earlier. But the bloody Russian repression, following so quickly on Blum's troubles and the constitutional crisis in London, seemed to make the opposition to Hitler and Mussolini weak indeed.

It is certain that the Government of Russia, concentrated in Stalin and the Politburo, was becoming more dictatorial and harsh, and that this Government, watching the rapid rise of Nazi might, was following a strictly realistic path. It was ruthlessly destroying all possible opponents at home. It was pushing an inexorable and feverish defense program, increasing its military expenditures (according to official figures) approximately forty times over, between 1932 and 1940. It was giving every impetus to industrial development as part of the defense program, and in the second Five-Year Plan, which ended in 1937, it paid special attention to forcing the growth of heavy industry.

At the same time, Russia was adopting a policy of pure opportunism in the avoidance of war. What the Soviet Union needed most was a long breathing space; what it feared most was a sudden German onslaught, acquiesced in if not encouraged by the Western democracies. To be sure, the Reich could not attack Russia while the Spanish struggle hung in the balance, while the power of France and Czechoslovakia (bound to Russia by rather vague pacts) was feared, and while Poland stood in the way. But Moscow from 1935 onward never ceased to flirt with the idea of negotiating with Berlin for a broad Russo-German understanding, and always contemplated the possibility that full collaboration with Germany, even in plans of joint conquest, might be advantageous. The British and French knew this, although they were horrified when open collaboration came. After the executions and purges of 1936–37, the governments in London, Paris, and Warsaw entertained no more faith in Russia than Russia entertained in them.

All this was highly unfortunate. The gulf between Britain and France on one side, Russia on the other, was by no means unbridgeable. In view of the fast-mounting strength of Germany and the unconcealed eagerness of both Hitler and Mussolini for conquests, it was most important that the peace-loving powers should band together to restrain the Fascist leaders. With more reason and tolerance in Moscow, more imagination and generosity in London and Paris, it might have been done. Instead, events in both the west and east of Europe broadened the misunderstanding.

But the mainspring of Anglo-French appeasement did not lie in political crises at home or in failure to achieve an understanding with Russia; it lay in the physical weakness of the two democracies, which failed lamentably to push rearmament with the determination that the time demanded. The Blum Government in September, 1936, announced with much fanfare a four-year

plan for putting about half a billion dollars into
armaments, whereas Germany was then spending
fully ten times that figure in a single year. The real
question, however, was of industrial preparedness.

The modern era of total war made full industrial mobilization the key to victory or defeat; and
the new power of highly mechanized devices rendered the *timing* of war equally important. The
nation which devoted three-fourths of its production to arms and munitions could fall with terrific
weight upon a nation which devoted only half its
resources to preparations for conflict. A totalitarian
state could obviously regiment its people for full
production much more easily than a democracy. It
could also do more to conceal its activities. Above
all, it could choose far in advance the precise
moment for its attack. By bending every effort to
devise superior airplanes, tanks, and heavy ordnance, it could bring these improved types into
mass production at just the moment chosen for
war.

It was this new element of timing which gave the
aggressor state its greatest advantage. Hitler knew
just when his armaments would be most overwhelmingly superior in design and mass to those of
his enemies, and could choose that moment to
strike. At the beginning of 1936 France and Britain
were far behind Germany in the number of their
first-line planes. What was much more significant

was the inferior quality of their aircraft, and the lack of facilities, especially in France, for continued airplane production.

The Roosevelt Administration did what seemed feasible to awaken the United States to its moral responsibilities, but this was at first little. In August, 1936, at Chautauqua, New York, the President issued a warning that neutrality laws were not enough. Americans, he said, were not isolationists "except in so far as we seek to isolate ourselves completely from war." Three weeks later Hull pointed to the gravity of the threat now overshadowing the globe. But it was the German outrages against civilization which did most to convince plain citizens that mere abstention from world affairs would never suffice. The intolerance of Hitler's regime appalled liberal peoples. A few decades earlier, Germany had been in the van of civilization; now she was adopting a barbarous attitude toward cultural and ethical values. The American press, pulpit, and public gatherings began to ring with denunciation. New York, with its large Jewish population, was the natural center of agitation. Liberal elements of the press denounced Nazi policy in savage terms. Every cruelty was reported, and the hidden truth about the concentration camps began to seep out. When on July 3, 1936, a Jewish journalist from Czechoslovakia committed suicide in the gallery of the League Assembly at Geneva, Americans understood that this symbolized the desperation of his people.

Anti-Nazi mass meetings became frequent. Unofficial boycotts of German goods were organized, often with the backing of organized labor as well as Jewish groups. After the explosion of the Zeppelin *Hindenburg*, Secretary Ickes refused to sanction helium exports to Germany to enable that country to resume use of its airships. However, this public reaction was spotty; and at the very time that popular indignation was finding scattered expression in mass meetings, boycotts, and official pinpricks—all regarded with contempt in Berlin, Rome, and Tokyo—the neutrality legislation was giving direct encouragement to the aggressors.

It was Japan which in 1937 opened the era of major aggressions. The decision which brought about the armed clash at the Marco Polo bridge near Peking on July 7, and thus began a conflict of staggering proportions, must be counted among the great turning points of this period. Back of this decision lay complex forces. The abortive attempt at a military coup in Tokyo in the "February 26 incident" had not produced a sharp reaction against the current domination of the government by the army and navy. Instead, the prestige of the armed forces was enhanced. The army by now believed that its mission was to regenerate Japan by bringing the people under rigid discipline, curbing private enterprise, and dictating economic and financial policy, while at the same time it led a heavily armed Japan along the path of territorial expansion.

Faced with this menacing thrust, the liberal forces in the Minseito and Seiyukai parties rallied, joined hands, and tried to make a last determined stand. At the general elections in the spring of 1937 they completely defeated the militarists and elected a heavy majority of the New Diet. But this availed them little. The army might suffer a temporary setback, but it recoiled only to leap farther ahead. Moreover, the Diet now counted for little, and the new Government proved singularly amenable to the wishes of the military clique. Its head was Prince Fumimaro Konoye, representative of a centuries-old house of great prestige; a man of only forty-five, whose early record in public life had been progressive and liberal. High hopes were reposed in him by believers in parliamentary institutions. But being a political pragmatist, with a shaky faith in democracy, he proved ready to experiment with totalitarian policies. From the outset he was enigmatic, and his natural pliability made him yield to the stern army pressures. The British Ambassador, who liked him for his brilliant personal traits, sums him up as a man of subtlety, knowledge of the world, breadth of vision—and vacillation. His Foreign Minister was Hirota, who had always stood close to army circles and did not displease them now. The War Minister, General Sugiyama, one of the Empire's best strategists, was a man of aggressive temper.

At the moment when the urbane, unprincipled and vacillating Konoye came to power, Japanese bayonets glistened all along the Great Wall of China; and the crucial question was whether they would attempt to pass it in force. By the spring of 1933, not only Manchukuo but the neighboring Jehol, corridor to Eastern Mongolia, had been effectively occupied. These were the outer fringes of the old Chinese Empire, and hope existed that China proper would be spared.

A continued state of sporadic warfare between Japan and China, however, had been inevitable ever since the conquest of Manchuria. No self-respecting Chinese Government could accept this loss of territory quietly, and retaliatory steps were natural: boycotts, border raids on Manchuria, and attempts to foment disturbances in that simmering area. As for the Japanese, they were caught in an iron frame which seemed to leave no choice but to go forward. No great country in the world was more dependent upon its export trade, and no important power relied upon so simple a list of export commodities: silk, cotton and rayon textiles, tea, and copper.

The silk industry having been hard hit by various factors, Japan had been forced to push her exports in other categories all the more frenziedly. The two great markets open to her were the United States and Asia, of which the latter offered much the greater promise of expansion. The teeming regions of southeastern Asia, with the neighboring islands, held perhaps a thousand million people; Japan understood their wants, and sympathized with their tastes; she believed that their low purchasing power might gradually be lifted. For a time the Japanese had hoped much from the Indian market, and had sold large quantities of cheap cotton textiles and silks there. But the Indian Government, encouraged by the British, had taken steps early in 1933 to raise the duties on textiles, meanwhile giving British manufacturers a decided preference. Throughout the British Empire, in fact, the Japanese were being accused of dumping their goods, and something like a British-Japanese economic war appeared in consequence. The Chinese market thus became more important than ever. As it did so, Japanese irritation over the stubborn opposition of many Chinese increased; the sense of injury over China's persistent boycotts grew more tense. The reasons, economic and strategic, for asserting some form of hegemony over East Asia became more compelling.

Hence not merely ambitious young officers but many businessmen were impatient to keep the

chariot of conquest rolling. Tokyo had been greatly
encouraged by the rise of Hitler and by Mussolini's
triumphant invasion of Ethiopia. The German idea
of *Lebensraum* and the general fascist concept of
economic autarchy touched a responsive chord in
the minds of countless Japanese. Resenting their
dependence for vital supplies on the United States,
the British Empire, and the Dutch, and eyeing
covetously the half-exploited riches rimming their
side of the Pacific, they hoped to make their country completely independent. They wished to move
southward on the Asiatic mainland step by step,
one encroachment paving the way for the next.
When that mainland was in their hands and they
possessed the oil, metals, rubber, and other resources for prolonged war—then they would plan
their next blow.

From the vantage point of Manchukuo and
Jehol, army officers had worked ceaselessly during
1933–36 to gain political and economic footholds
in northern China. They had helped set up what
they hoped would prove a puppet government in
Peking, ruling the five northern provinces. Actually, however, this government exhibited a dis-
concerting readiness to act with other Chinese
elements, including Chiang Kai-shek, rather than
with Tokyo. The principal Japanese agent was
Colonel Doihara, who had helped pull the strings in
the Mukden incident. This indefatigable militarist

leader returned from a tour into North China in 1935 with a scheme for the creation of a great bloc comprehending Japan, Manchukuo, and the five North Chinese provinces. The mines, fisheries, and agricultural products of this area, controlled from Tokyo, would go far toward making Japan impregnable. Doihara's plan was set aside as premature, but his activities continued; and in his path there always sprang up an immediate crop of local dissensions and an ultimate harvest of Japanese garrisons. As Japanese intrigues grew more provocative, Chinese anger mounted until an explosive situation emerged.

The match was set to the powder train when in early July, 1937, a body of Japanese troops carrying out maneuvers near Peking (an irregular proceeding) came into contact with a Chinese force. A night engagement with light casualties was followed by a heavier affray at the Marco Polo bridge. This gave the Japanese army a double opportunity: it could press forward with the deglutition of the northern provinces, and it could stir up a war fever at home which would put the troublesome Diet in its place and consolidate the power of the direct-actionists.

The Sino-Japanese War had begun. It was expected to last but a few months, when the chastened Chiang Kai-shek and his northern followers would treat for peace. The Konoye Cabinet sought at once to restrict the scope of the collision. But in reality the conflict was to call forth almost the full strength of the Japanese army, to require at times a million men, to cost a mountain of treasure, and to stretch down the years until it merged with a greater and more frightful war. What was to be an "incident," permitting the cheap detachment of a northern segment of the republic, became a challenge to all Japan's strength and tenacity.

The reason for this lay in the decision of Chinese leaders that the time had come to fight to the last, and in their ability to make that determination good. Both Tokyo and the West underestimated the cohesive strength of China. The National Government was led by the shrewd, albeit unprincipled, and often exasperatingly shifty statesman who was also a masterly strategist, Chiang Kai-shek. It possessed a powerful and well-balanced if ill-equipped army. It had succeeded in coming to a general understanding with the Hopei-Chahar Provincial Council in Peking. By one blow after another, by a long succession of affronts, by outrage piled on outrage, the Japanese had welded a greater unity in China than they realized. The northern government, which had its own army and collected its own taxes, had long been frigidly aloof from Chiang, but now was ready to act in close cooperation.

Fighting rapidly spread over a great part of China. Heavy Japanese reinforcements were poured into the northern area, and Tientsin and Peking were occupied before the close of July. Hostilities began in the Shanghai area on August 13. After bloody grappling, the Japanese gained full possession and pushed inland toward Nanking. They seized that Chinese capital before 1937 ended, and then controlled much of eastern China. But "control" was a dubious word, for they were rather mired down in the great hostile land, subjected to ceaseless guerrilla attacks. Every effort to bring the Hopei-Chahar Council or Chiang Kai-shek to terms failed, for both refused to yield.

Thus involved in a far heavier struggle than it had expected, and aware that further penetration meant simply greater difficulties, the army grew reckless. It treated foreign interests in China—the French, Americans, Italians, and British—with insolence and brusqueness. In the home islands, the war placed enhanced power in the hands of extremists. The China war thus advanced Japan far along the path of an ultimate clash with the Western powers. The heightened tension in American relations was immediately evident. With great commercial, religious, and educational interests in China, the United States had about 3,000 citizens in the Shanghai area alone. Meanwhile, China on September 12 appealed to the League Council.

Just after the Marco Polo clash, Secretary Hull issued a resounding manifesto on American foreign policy modeled upon his general declaration at the Buenos Aires conference in 1936, sending it to foreign governments for comment. He began with the truism that any situation which threatened or created war was a situation which affected the interests of all nations. Litvinov had summed up the idea more concisely in saying that peace is indivisible. Hull went on to assert that the United States advocated a long line of principles: maintenance of peace, abstinence from the use of force, non-interference with foreign nations, treaty observance, revitalization of international law, promotion of international security and stability, lowering of trade barriers, equality of commercial opportunity and limitation of armaments. The republic, he concluded, would avoid alliances or entangling commitments, but believed in cooperative effort to sustain the principles stated.

Hull might have added that America did not believe in cooperation intensely enough to take any real risks in its behalf. The Comic Spirit must have smiled over the replies which came from Germany, Italy, and Japan. Berlin smacked unctuous lips over the statement that its "basic principle is, as is generally known, directed toward the regulation of international relations by pacific agreement."

Italy replied that it favored everything which assisted the pacification of the world. Tokyo expressed concurrence in Hull's fine ideas, but remarked that such objectives would be attained in the Far East only by practical consideration of the actual circumstances found in that area of the globe!

What could the United States do? It could and did reinforce the 2,500 Marines and infantry in China by sending out 1,200 more men. It could offer its good offices in settling the Sino-Japanese quarrel, as Great Britain did; but Japan refused any response to our informal approaches. Hull could scold Ambassador Saito; he could instruct Grew to expostulate and to warn Japan. Ambassador Grew, in fact, used blunt language. When he learned on September 20 that the Japanese were planning to bomb Nanking, he hastened to give Foreign Minister Hirota an emphatic talk, reminding him that pacific and patient though Americans were, they became under provocation the most inflammable people on the planet. Despite the warning, Japanese air attacks on Nanking, Canton, Hangkow, and other cities resulted in hideous loss of life. But though Grew admonished Japan of "the steadily mounting feeling" in the United States, he had no means of reaching the military leaders who dominated the government. Washington cooperated broadly with London, but on parallel lines, avoiding that joint action which might unduly incense Tokyo.

For obvious reasons, the United States was anxious not to apply the Neutrality Act. While Japan manufactured large quantities of munitions, China produced but little. An embargo would therefore damage the Chinese cause much more heavily than the Japanese. The fact that Japan, while fighting on a large scale, stubbornly denied that she was at war, gave Washington an excuse for not proclaiming a state of hostilities. After several White House conferences, Roosevelt in September declared that the Neutrality Act was not being invoked, and that merchant ships under the American flag could take war merchandise to China or Japan at their own risk. This met with popular approval. As long as no formal state of war existed, Japan could not declare a blockade of China and ships could move freely. The situation was precisely the reverse of that in the Ethiopian War, when the Government had been glad to apply the Neutrality Act because it would hamper the aggressor. A meeting under League auspices of the Far East Advisory Committee (created after the Lytton Report on the crisis in Manchuria), with an American representative present but not voting, early in October condemned Japan's acts as a violation of the Nine-Power Treaty and the Kellogg-Briand Pact.

Both Roosevelt and Hull, realizing that aggression in the East was linked with aggression in the West, felt deeply the threat to all civilization; and the new crisis evoked one of the President's most famous (and most impetuous) utterances, the "quarantine speech" in Chicago on October 5, 1937. He described at length the anxious situation in international affairs. An era of lawlessness, he said, had set in; the foundations of the liberal world were threatened; and nobody should harbor the delusion that the United States could escape the general menace. If America dallied, the Western Hemisphere would in time be attacked. The one means by which orderly nations could preserve a decent world was to act in concert to uphold the principles sustaining peace. "War is contagion, be it declared or undeclared. It can engulf states and peoples remote from the original scene of hostilities." The peace-loving nations, including the United States, should quarantine war so effectively that any power tempted to violate the rights of other peoples would desist.

"America," concluded Roosevelt, "hates war. America hopes for peace. Therefore, America actively engages in the search for peace." This bold effort to awaken public opinion overshot the mark, for its rash phrases frightened people who feared that the country might be dragged into a new cauldron of battle. It had a bad press, and set back the cause of public education instead of advancing it. But even if it had met warm support, the speech would have availed little. A League with America in it, enforcing the economic sanctions for which the Covenant provided, might well have stopped aggression without precipitating a major conflict; now it was too late.

This fact was demonstrated by the conference of signatories of the Nine-Power Treaty which, in an atmosphere of impotence if not defeatism, took place in Brussels in November. The gathering was called by the League on the very day of Roosevelt's speech, and representatives of eighteen nations attended. Shrewd observers expected little from it. It was clear that the Nine-Power Treaty had been violated by Japan, but it was also clear that Japan defied the world. Apart from offering China moral support, the conferees had a choice of only three roads. They could follow the United States and Britain in suggesting mediation—which Japan would reject. They could brand Japan as an aggressor nation, which would simply harden the temper of the Japanese miltarists. They could, finally, adopt economic sanctions against Japan— if they cared to risk a war in which Germany and Italy might well join. Roosevelt had made it plain that the United States would not tread the third path when he instructed the American delegate, Norman H. Davis, that while Washington believed in cooperative effort to preserve peace by pacific means, "public opinion in the United States has expressed its emphatic determination that the United States keep out of war."

With Japan refusing to attend the Brussels conference and adopting an attitude of sharp hostility toward it—the very phrase "Nine-Power Conference" seemed to Tokyo to suggest pressure by eight nations upon the ninth—the value of the conference was dubious. Its pious regrets and affirmations of faith in peace struck the world as an exercise in weary futility. Its invitation to Japan to settle her differences with China brought a mind-your-own-business response. Observers in Tokyo felt that it left the Government there more obstinate than before. It perhaps had some value in showing the eight protesting nations that they must give China all the economic and financial assistance within their power. It also perhaps did something to educate American opinion, proving that Britain and France would go just as far to help the United States in the Far East as the United States would go in helping Britain and France in Europe. In more senses than one, peace was indivisible.

How deeply American feeling was still committed to isolationism was illustrated by the *Panay* incident of December 12, 1937. Early in December a battery of field artillery, commanded by one of

the most ruthless of the young Japanese officers,
deliberately shelled the British gunboats *Bee* and
Ladybird. Immediately thereafter, Japanese aircraft bombed and sank the American gunboat
Panay on the Yangtse above Nanking, and with
it three merchant vessels of the United States. A
number of Americans were killed. Some survivors,
including wounded, who attempted to crawl into a
thicket on shore, were machine-gunned. It was
clear that the Japanese had seen the American
flag displayed on the gunboat. For a short time
Grew feared that another "Remember the *Maine*"
wave would sweep America.

But the Japanese did much to soften American
anger when Foreign Minister Hirota called immediately at the Embassy to express profound regret, while the navy took the unprecedented step
of making a similar apology. Never was an incident
more quickly closed. The attack took place on the
12th, an American demand for apology, indemni-
fication, and assurances for the future was delivered on the 13th, and the Japanese Minister was
at the Embassy doorstep with humble words on
the 14th. Inquiry showed that the orders to bomb
the *Panay* had come from a Colonel Hashimoto,
prominent in a clique of young officers who had
previously been involved in an unsuccessful military conspiracy; and that the Japanese Government protested that it had not been directly re-

sponsible in any way. By an adroit arrangement, the formal Japanese accession to all American requirements was delivered in Washington on Christmas Eve, while acceptance of the apology was dispatched on Christmas afternoon. Hirota's eyes filled with tears as he read it. When a few months later the United States presented a claim of two million dollars, Tokyo promptly paid it. The Japanese Government had expressed a fervent hope that the "unfortunate affair" would not cloud the friendly relations between the two countries. Whether it had or not, it was evident that it had deepened the flood of isolationist feeling. Except in some resentful naval circles, unqualified relief was expressed over the pacific settlement of the affair.

America, many believed, should take steps to get out of the Orient and stay out—take out every missionary, merchant, soldier, sailor, tourist, educator. In 1934, moved partly by idealistic considerations, partly by a desire to reduce overseas commitments, and most of all by the selfish wish to get rid of an embarrassing competitor in the domestic marketing of certain agricultural products, Congress had passed an act for granting full independence to the Philippines in 1946. A demand was now arising in some quarters that the Act should take effect immediately. It was generally recognized that the islands were non-defensible if Japan ever chose to attack in force. The fortress of Corregidor at the gate of Manila Bay had been given great strength, but it could at most resist but a few months, while all the rest of the archipelago could be rapidly overrun. Why not sever so exposed an outpost at once? some Americans asked. Congress was resolutely declining to fortify Guam or extend its air fields. That little island, too, would therefore fall an easy prey to Japanese sea power.

There could be no question that many Nipponese naval officers believed that all the Western powers should and would be driven out of the Far Eastern area. They could find it stated in authoritative American books that the naval ratio of the United States and Japan in 1937–39 was not five to three, but merely five to four; and this of course left Japan temporarily impregnable. The Senate in January, 1938, asked Secretary Hull to inform it how many American nationals lived in China, what American capital was invested there, and how large were the military and naval forces there; a request which drew from the Secretary a tart statement that something far more important than money was involved—the principle "that orderly processes in international relationships be maintained." That same month a Gallup poll showed that 70 per cent of the cross-section of population questioned believed that total withdrawal from the Orient was desirable.

Such a figure was not impressive. The question was badly phrased. Offhand, many people when asked about getting citizens and investments out of an area boiling with trouble would approve the step. A query whether legitimate American interests in the Orient should be abandoned because of Japanese pressure might have brought a very different response. But it was significant that four months earlier only 54 per cent had voted for withdrawal. Moreover, in this same January the House failed by only thirty-one votes to adopt the beforementioned Ludlow amendment requiring that a popular referendum precede any declaration of war. Any schoolboy could see that, in an international crisis demanding quick and decisive action, such a law might fatally cripple the republic. Yet it almost passed one chamber. On the surface, isolationism seemed strong as ever.

Not, however, beneath the surface, where the deeper tides of national sentiment are registered. The heroic resistance of China was stirring countless hearts. The Ethiopians had fought against aggression; so had the Spanish loyalists; but most heartening of all was the fight which renascent China, the bulkiest, most peaceful, and till lately most inert of nations, was waging. It had apparently been a veritable jellyfish; but a succession of leaders, first Sun Yat-sen, founder of the republic of 1911, then Yuan Shi-kai, Dictator-

President during the First World War, and later
Chiang Kai-shek, had builded better than the outside world knew. A national spirit had arisen; a
generation of men and women intent on the re-
generation of their ancient land had sprung up.
Bleeding at a hundred veins, China grew weaker
but refused to be broken. Japanese columns pene-
trated far into the interior, and could hold most
of the principal towns, but the countrysides remained hostile; communications grew precarious,
and troops wasted away in a relentless guerrilla
warfare.

Japan's heavy air raids upon Canton in the
spring of 1938 were murderously terroristic. That
city, strongly held by Chinese forces, was an invaluable port. If it and its northward communications could be seized, Chiang Kai-shek's armies
would have to fall back into the interior, using
only the French railroad from Indo-China to
Kunming, the Burma Road, and the arteries with
Soviet Russia. To land an expeditionary force
adequate to the task would, however, have been a
costly operation. Hence, day after day, and frequently several times a day, the Japanese rained
bombs upon the flimsy, crowded, defenseless city.

Casualties ran high into the thousands. Correspondents reported that Sun Yat-sen University
outside the city, pride and hope of young China,
was a special target. The Mayor made a moving

appeal to all free cities throughout the world. Protest meetings were held in Britain and France. Secretary Welles on June 3, thinking both of Spain and China, declared that the bombing of civil populations was barbarous. It was notorious to onlookers at Canton that, as an American correspondent wrote, "this daily slaughter of innocent non-combatants . . . was largely being accomplished with materials furnished by American companies for a price." To end this reproach, the State Department on July 1, 1938, informed manufacturers and exporters of aircraft that the Government was strongly opposed to shipments which would assist indiscriminate bombings; and that it would issue export licenses "with great regret." This moral embargo effectively halted the transfer of planes to Japan.

The China incident had now become the China war. Japan's resources were being heavily strained; her reputation before the world had been blackened by Nanking and Canton. The Government in Tokyo had to be remodeled again, and it again became more extremist in character. The army insisted that, since Japan recognized no civil government in China, Foreign Minister Hirota had no concern with affairs there. He gave way, in the face of these demands, to a general who held office for four months, whereupon Prime Minister Konoye himself took control of foreign relations. In his pliable fashion, Konoye quickly yielded to the extremists, granting the army full control over Japan's policy toward China. Henceforth no curb could be applied to the policies and operations of the armed forces in China. The emotions of humane and liberal peoples all over the world were becoming deeply aroused. In the fall of 1937 the A. F. of L. and the C.I.O. passed resolutions against the export of goods to Japan; and meanwhile, a popular boycott of Japanese wares made steady progress in America.

Roosevelt was now pushing the rearmament of the United States with farsighted energy and acumen, and the support he received pointed to a certain change in the national psychology The country was beginning to think that Germany and Japan might become its deadly enemies. In a special message at the end of January, 1938, the President declared that other powers were arming themselves "at an unprecedented and alarming rate," and that although a great majority of the human race wished to live in peace, one-fourth of the population of the globe was plunged in "merciless devastating conflict." He informed Congress that the national defenses were inadequate and must be boldly increased. Both coasts might be attacked at once, he intimated, and cities far in the interior of the country could be raided by bombers. Actually, as early as 1938, according to subsequent revelations at Nuremberg, Goering called for planes that would be able to bomb New York. The President asked for a larger army, an increase of one-fifth in the current construction program, and funds to begin two additional battleships and two new cruisers during 1938. Some opposition sprang up in pacifist and isolationist quarters, which suggested that a secret agreement for naval cooperation with Great Britain had been reached. Secretary Hull at once came to the President's aid with a categorical denial, and an assertion that if the United States kept its armed forces weak, this would encourage lawless and predatory nations. The Roosevelt program was adopted by Congress without substantial change.

Already the Administration, with Secretary Morgenthau in the van, was paying attention to two vital concomitants of defense: systematic assistance to Britain and France in obtaining certain weapons, notably advanced types of aircraft, that only the United States could supply, and the accumulation of stock piles of essential raw materials. As head of the Treasury, Mr. Morgenthau was responsible for procurement of all Government supplies. It was natural for him to use the Procurement Division to assist the British and French purchasing missions which reached the United States in 1938, and also to lay up stocks of rare metals needed in defense activities. From the end of 1937 Morgenthau was head of the Administration elements pressing for energetic resistance of Hitler, Mussolini, and the Japanese warlords, just as Secretary of War Woodring was head of the isolationist group within Roosevelt's immediate following. But Morgenthau was in a position to influence the President and to reach public sentiment; Woodring was not.

Then in the spring of 1938 another thunderclap shook Europe. Hitler's sudden occupation of Austria greatly augmented the wealth and manpower at his command, increased his arrogant confidence in his star, rendered the position of Czechoslovakia, now surrounded on three sides, highly precarious, and heightened the tension reigning throughout the world.

It is unnecessary to rehearse in detail the story of the absorption of Austria. In 1935 Hitler had publicly avowed that he had no desire to annex the little country, or even to conclude an economic union with her, and that he would not interfere in her internal affairs. The next year he signed a treaty promising to respect the "full sovereignty" of Austria, which might deal with Austrian Nazis as it pleased. But the beginning of 1938 found him perfecting a plot against his weak neighbor: a riot was to be provoked in Vienna, the German army was to march across the border to restore order, and Austria was to become part of the Reich. The plot was discovered by the Viennese police. Hitler had to turn to other methods. Then came the invitation to Chancellor Schuschnigg to visit the Fuehrer at Berchtesgaden; the brutal order that he must admit Nazis to key positions in his Cabinet; Schuschnigg's compliance; his desperate attempt to retard German annexation by calling for a plebiscite on the question of union; Hitler's peremptory interference to forbid any such election, which would result in an anti-Nazi victory; the forced resignation of Schuschnigg in favor of Hitler's tool, Arthur Seyss-Inquart; and the new Chancellor's announcement over the radio: "Austria is free! One people, one Reich, one leader! Heil Hitler!" On March 12, German troops occupied Vienna, and two days later Hitler made a triumphant entry into that city.

The shocked world could do nothing. The Italian people had much to fear from the fact that the Nazis now faced them across the Brenner Pass; but since the formation of the Rome-Berlin Axis in the fall of 1936, and still more since the adherence of Italy the following year to the Berlin-Tokyo Anti-Comintern Pact, Mussolini was helpless. Other European nations could not interfere. After all, the people of Austria were of German blood; some of them had wished for this union; the rest had passively complied. But just the same, the brutality of Hitler's tactics, the numbing power of the *blitz* which he turned upon Austria, grieved and angered all democratic opinion.

Secretary Hull well expressed the feeling of countless reflective Americans. The vital question, he said in a speech of March 17, was whether the doctrine of brute force would again prevail in the world, or whether the peace-loving powers could act to maintain law, order, and justice as the foundation of civilized relations among nations. Could the United States (as Father Coughlin, Senator Langer, and others really wished) turn its back on the tragic situation, and leave the Old World to shift for itself? It could—but at a fearful price. It would have to give up its championship of principles on which its people had always believed that true civilization and progress must rest: democracy, representative self-government, tolerance, equal justice before the law. It must abandon its historic association with like-minded nations; and as they saw the United States surrender its legitimate interests abroad, their attitude toward the republic would change from amity to frigidity. America would be left without a friend in a world of enemies. Without markets abroad, compelled to arm to the teeth to protect itself, it would have to reshape the entire economic and social structure of the country, dropping to lower living standards and accepting a regimentation in which liberty would perish. Nor would even this bring security;

isolation, said Hull, "is a fruitful source of insecurity."

Many Americans were beginning to wonder whether isolationism was in fact not the most perilous of all paths. One nation after another had now been conquered by Fascism—Ethiopia, Spain, Austria. By his latest victory Hitler had added seven millions to the population of the Reich, obtained valuable timber, iron ore, and magnesite holdings, augmented his stock of gold and of foreign securities, and gained important new business connections with southeastern Europe. Where would the march end? Secretary Hull had told the Canadian Minister that Germany was "bent on becoming the dominating colossus of continental Europe." And after Europe? It would be easier, numerous Americans began to suspect, to stop the redoubtable Axis while strong allies were available than after they had all been struck down.

Many Americans began to feel a deep apprehension, moreover, regarding the sway which the two great totalitarian cults of Nazism and Communism were establishing over weak-minded or perverted groups in the population. Under Nazi inspiration, a body called the German-American Bund was founded in the United States, which with Fritz Kuhn as leader enjoyed a rapid growth among discontented or un-Americanized elements of German blood. It scattered local units throughout the North and West, published a newspaper called the *Deutscher Weckruff und Beobachter*, and in 1938 operated twenty-two summer camps which combined exercise, drill, and Nazi "hot-gospelling." Part of the German language press in the United States showed distinct sympathy with Nazi aims. Meanwhile, the Communists recruited many followers among writers, artists, teachers, and other intellectuals (often in the sense that an intellectual is to an intelligent man as a gent is to a gentleman), dominated the critical and colored the political columns of some radical weeklies, and made a special appeal to underpaid workingmen, Negroes, and to devotees of change for change's sake. They also had their publications, the chief of which was the *Daily Worker* in New York. They looked to Moscow as the Bund looked to Berlin. Millions of Americans had accepted the existence of such alien-led and alien-used organizations with tolerance so long as their foreign affiliations did not seem dangerous. But now that Nazi Germany was a great and menacing power, they began to feel that tolerance had limits.

By the summer of 1938 the great rally in America against the aggressor nations was gaining momentum. That summer saw the tension between Germany and Czechoslovakia steadily increasing. Early autumn brought a crisis which marked the turning point in democratic sentiment the world over. After Munich, true lovers of peace in France, Britain, and America saw that appeasement would not do; that the only safety lay in preparations, urgent and furious, for resistance. The sands were running out. Civilization stood on the brink of dangers that might engulf it.

CHAPTER VI

By the spring of 1938 American interest in international affairs had become painfully intense. To some, the fantastic scene was simply a grandiose panorama to be watched with the aid of foreign correspondents, columnists, and radio commentators. But to many millions it compelled a grimmer attention: it affected the value of steel and copper, wheat and cotton, machines and fabrics; it raised or depressed the price of stocks, accentuated or lightened the depression. Above all, it threatened the future of the rising generation. Events made it plain that Germany, Italy, and Japan were linked in a loose partnership, each profiting from the pressure exerted by the others. The times seemed marching toward some great catastrophe. And if 1914 repeated itself, how long would it be before the United States again faced the ineluctable choice of 1917?

Every word of Hitler now resounded around the

world, and the United States took careful note of his speech of February 19, 1938, to the German Reichstag. It had laid down a program menacing the future existence of Czechoslovakia no less than Austria. More than ten million Germans, declared Hitler, lived in two states adjoining the Reich's frontiers. "Till 1866 they were constitutionally united with the whole German people." (The fact was that the Czechs, and the Sudeten Germans in Czechoslovakia, had never been part of Germany, but had been included in the Austro-Hungarian Monarchy.) These people, he went on, had a right to the self-determination promised in Wilson's Fourteen Points. "In the long run it is intolerable for a self-respecting world power to be deprived of its entity, and to know that across the frontier are kinsmen who have to suffer severe persecution simply because of their sympathy, their feeling of union, and their common point of view with the whole German people." When he united the seven million Austrians with their German brethren, his words regarding the Sudeten Germans were recalled with dark foreboding.

Could Czechoslovakia be preserved? Americans were discussing that question in the spring of 1938, aware that the crisis would probably come in early autumn. The question vitally concerned three powers friendly to the Czechs: France, which had a military alliance with them; Britain, which was bound to fight if France did; and Russia. All three were weak in fighting power, and all possessed uncertain policies and unreliable leadership. France had in September, 1938, only about seven hundred airplanes of all types, with not a single up-to-date bomber, and no reserve planes; while her production rate was under forty machines a month! In February, 1939, only forty-four were turned out, and in March, thirty-five. Anti-aircraft defenses were practically non-existent except in Paris, and weak there. Yet Germany had large aircraft reserves, and a monthly production of approximately five hundred planes. In tanks the French position was equally pitiable. Midsummer of 1938 found the republic with only thirty-four modern tanks, far inferior in design to Germany's powerful equipment; while the French were almost without anti-tank guns.

A great French rearmament program had been decided upon in September, 1936, when the Cabinet council voted to spend fourteen billion francs (increased later to twenty billion) for planes, tanks, and other material. Militarily, France was to be raised to the German level. So huge was the program that it involved the complete rebuilding of French industry. But the social legislation of 1936, the work primarily of Leon Blum, was now in force: the forty-hour week, paid holidays, the plans for transferring armament factories to the state. These reforms, sound in principle, had unfortunate effects in practice. The fact was that, as André Geraud later wrote in *The Gravediggers of France*, the nation stood on the brink of revolution. Her masses were barely held under control, and Communist and other agitators would have thrust the country into the abyss had not tremendous concessions been made. The efficiency of industry was sharply impaired. Indeed, at the gravest crisis in French and European history, two years were largely lost. Part of the responsibility must be placed on the industrialists, for the sit-down strikes, the social reforms, and the nationalization of armament plants made many manufacturers sullenly uncooperative.

Russia had no common boundary with Czechoslovakia and could have given help only by moving armed forces through, and air fleets over, Poland, Hungary, or Rumania. All these nations were timorous in facing Germany; the Poles and Hungarians, eager to obtain Czech territory, rather sympathized with Hitler's plans. Probably they would have resisted any Russian march. No one knew how greatly the Soviet Union had been weakened by the recent trials and executions, but most observers believed that the shooting of Marshall Tukhachevsky and other high officers had struck a grievous blow to Russia's forces. The early weeks of 1938 found Bukharin and other conspicuous leaders being sentenced to the death penalty, and the "liquidations" continued all summer. Moreover, it was questionable whether Russian promises of assistance to France and Czechoslovakia would have been kept to any material extent. A few airplane flights would have availed little. As for Great Britain, while her navy was powerful, her army was insignificant, and her air fleet was just coming into existence. Nothing could have prevented Hitler's rapid conquest of Czechoslovakia had war once begun.

In leadership, also, the opposition to Hitler was exceedingly weak. In the near future, Britain was to produce one of the most inspiring statesmen of her long history, but his hour had not yet struck. Prime Minister Neville Chamberlain was a conscientious, cautious, and overcredulous businessman, who hated war and believed that by careful bargaining he could reach an agreement with the dictators. His principal advisers, Sir John Simon and Samuel Hoare, were men of his own pattern; Simon a little sly, Hoare a little arrogant. Neither had been a success at the Foreign Office. Chamberlain was pursuing a double policy of preparedness and appeasement. On one hand, plans for the complete rearmament of Britain had been drafted as early as 1935, and were being efficiently worked out. On the other hand, while the United Kingdom remained weak and was faced by the combined

threat of Germany and Italy in the West and
Japan in the Far East, Chamberlain thought it
necessary to purchase time by conciliatory tactics.
He hoped that if Germany were allowed only those
gains to which she was morally entitled she would
prove content. He did not perceive that Hitler had
made up his mind to dominate first Europe, and
then the world.

French leadership was even weaker than British,
and French disunity had become so deep that many
observers (including Hitler) had anticipated civil
war in the fall of 1936. Blum had fallen when in
June, 1937, the Senate refused him power to decree
any measure needed to restore the national finances.
He had been succeeded by Camille Chautemps, an
amiable weakling, who gave way in the spring of
1938 to Edouard Daladier, a forcible-feeble figure
whose conservatism made him suspicious of Communism and friendly to Fascism. French finances
remained alarmingly weak. The quarrels between
Communists and reactionaries were savage and
irreconcilable. While the Left, strongly oriented
toward Moscow, believed that the Right was intent on reducing the working classes to slavery, the
Right held that open conquest by Hitler and Mussolini might be preferable to covert conquest by
Communist ideas. Under Chautemps and Daladier,
the pact with Russia had been reduced to a mere
shadow. Daladier's Foreign Minister, Georges Bon-

net, was intensely distrustful of Russia and in favor of an accommodation with the Reich. Moreover, the army itself was gravely divided, while peasants and workmen, recalling the sacrifices in 1914–18, were willing to take almost any future risk to avoid an immediate war.

As for Russia, her leadership remained the great enigma. "There are indications," wrote Ambassador Davies on March 17, 1938, "that this government is going more isolationist than ever before." Litvinov told Davies frankly that "France has no confidence in the Soviet Union, and the Soviet Union has no confidence in France." Relations with Poland were so seriously strained that had Warsaw pushed her demands on Lithuania in the spring of 1938 much further, war might have resulted. Relations with Rumania were equally difficult.

The situation was complicated for both France and Britain by the moral dubiety of the Sudetenland issue, and for Britain by the necessity of consulting Dominion sentiment. The Czech Government had not treated generously the minorities placed within its bounds, all of whom had valid complaints. To go to war to prevent Sudeten Germans from joining the Fatherland would be to take a delicate responsibility at the bar of history. It would in particular have been a serious matter for Britain to ask Canadians, Australians, New Zealanders, and South Africans to lay down their lives in such a cause. An Imperial Conference in 1937 had shown that the Dominions would go to almost any extreme to avoid involvement in a new European conflict.

So it was that the world watched with bated breath an intricate and fateful drama, sure to reach its denouement before fall of 1938; and the American public took the interest of spectators who knew they might soon become participants.

On the ground that Germany was massing troops on the frontier, the Czechs ordered army maneuvers during the night of May 20. On May 29, Hitler publicly called for expansion of his army and air force and for rushing the western fortifications to completion, saying that "a great power cannot accept a second time such a mean assault." Throughout the summer extra labor forces toiled on the West Wall. On August 15 the Reich army began extensive maneuvers, while Berlin took other steps which seemed a direct preparation for war. Reservists were called up, recruits were held over for extra service, and the army command was given power to requisition civilian goods and services. When the British Ambassador protested, Von Ribbentrop refused to discuss the subject. Announcement that the British fleet would hold September maneuvers north of Scotland brought the defiant retort from Germany that its warships would hold September maneuvers in the North Sea.

In mid-September something closely approaching a national mobilization of Germany took place. To celebrate the Party Day at Nuremberg, one and a half million Nazis gathered in and about the ancient city. The theme of the celebration was Greater Germany. To the cheering multitudes it was announced that the Sudeten Germans would have a very special Party Day on October 15—a virtual boast that by that hour they would be "liberated." At the same time, the military forces of the Reich mobilized under arms were increased to fully 1,500,000, while a clamor of warlike preparations filled the areas behind the border encampments. With the whole nation standing at attention, poised to march, the Fuehrer delivered his much-anticipated speech on the climactic day at Nuremberg, September 12. He pictured the Sudeten Germans as suffering intolerable wrongs; declared that, "if these tortured creatures cannot obtain rights and assistance by themselves, they can obtain both from us"; and laid down a categorical demand—"I insist that the oppression of three and a half million Germans in Czechoslovakia shall cease and yield to a free self-determination."

Was Hitler bluffing? Would he, if firmly defied, have drawn back? It is impossible to say, but it seems unlikely. Subsequent German statements that he would have yielded if Britain, France, and Russia had confronted him with determined mien must be taken with reserve. Von Ribbentrop and others who said this at the post-war trials had every reason for trying to place the blame for the Second World War on Chamberlain, Bonnet, and other democratic leaders. Hitler himself was ready to boast later, when some advisers thought he risked too much, "See what I won by just bluffing." The fact was that he had thirty divisions on the Czech and other frontiers, that five hundred airplanes were ready to attack, that he had blocked the negotiations between the Czech Government and Sudeten leaders, and that his and Goering's speeches at Nuremberg had raised grave disorders in the Sudetenland. He could not draw back without ruinous humiliation. Evidence has been presented that a group of officers led by General Beck, Chief of the German General Staff, was ready for a military coup to overthrow Hitler when the surrender at Munich destroyed their plans. But the dismally ineffective history of German opposition to Hitler suggests that this coup might never have taken place, or might have failed.

A series of hectic events led up to a dramatic climax. Chamberlain, taking his pride in his hands, flew on September 15 to Berchtesgaden to talk with Hitler in the hope of finding a peaceful solution. Receiving Hitler's terms, he returned to London to consult with his Cabinet, Premier Daladier, and Foreign Minister Bonnet. Gaining their consent to the Fueher's demands, he went back to Germany on September 22 for a second conference at Godesberg. But Hitler, instead of accepting a settlement on the lines he had previously indicated, now raised his demands to a more exorbitant level. Chamberlain bitterly upbraided him for his failure to respond to the unprecedented efforts of Britain and France to maintain peace, and departed for home in despairing disgust. London and Paris at once notified the Czechs that they should mobilize; the Czech army was called to the colors; the French Government brought another half-million men under arms, making a million in all; and Chamberlain declared that if war came, Britain would support France. Meanwhile, the British Mediterranean fleet had been made ready for action, air-raid shelters had been prepared, and gas-masks had been distributed in London.

The United States was watching the situation with intense anxiety, and its Government was eager to help avert hostilities. As news came of Chamberlain's rebuff, Roosevelt took a hand. In the early stages of the crisis he had held cautiously aloof, suspecting that Chamberlain might try to maneuver America into a position where partial responsibility for the choice between war and appeasement would rest upon her shoulders. The

President was determined to keep this responsibility squarely upon the British and French Governments. But by September 26 the danger of a new world-wide conflict was such that some action was inescapable. The disclosure of Hitler's new terms had shocked American sentiment. Obviously, Roosevelt could not promise to use American troops and money, for the nation's interests were not vitally involved. He could not gain anything by railing at Hitler, or by scolding the two unhappy prime ministers, caught in a tragic dilemma. His one possible course was to make a fervent plea for peace.

Chamberlain, after his return from Godesberg and the intensification of preparations for war, made a last-minute plea to Hitler for a resumption of negotiations, with Czech delegates included. Before this letter was delivered, Roosevelt sent Hitler and Benes a message upon which he and Hull had labored for half the night of September 25–26. Peace in Europe if not throughout the world, they wrote, was in immediate danger. "The consequences of the rupture are incalculable. Should hostilities break out the lives of millions of men, women and children . . . will certainly be lost under circumstances of unspeakable horror. The economic system of every country involved is certain to be shattered." Speaking for America and humanity in general, they pleaded for a continuance of negotiations looking to a peaceful, fair, and constructive settlement. The Czechs, British, and French at once cabled their assent. Hitler, however, replied in a refractory vein. He dispatched on the 27th a virtual rejection. After accusing the Czech regime of violence and terrorism, he declared that a settlement could no longer be postponed, and that it was for the leaders at Prague alone to decide whether they wanted peace or war. Instantly, Roosevelt sent the Fueher a second appeal, dated September 27, suggesting an immediate conference of all interested nations at some neutral spot—to which no reply whatever was vouchsafed.

At the same time, both Roosevelt and Chamberlain called upon Mussolini to use his good offices. The Prime Minister asked the Duce to consent to a conference, and to persuade Hitler to join it; a shrewd move, for it catered to Mussolini's vanity by enabling him to play a major role, while Hitler would find it easier to yield to his partner than to anyone else. Roosevelt on the evening of the 27th transmitted a message which was handed to Mussolini the following morning. It thus came under the Duce's eye at almost the same moment that Chamberlain's appeal was delivered by Lord Perth.

The last sands now seemed running out. All Europe expected war within a few hours. The German Government, according to its own statement, had fixed the invasion of Czechoslovakia for 2 P.M.

that day. Mussolini hurriedly instructed his Ambassador in Berlin to ask that the action which Hitler had threatened that afternoon be postponed for at least twenty-four hours to permit a reexamination of the question. The response was all that could be desired. Hitler was ready to grant the postponement. Then he telephoned in the early afternoon that he would agree to the conference and wished Mussolini to attend it at Munich the following day. Possibly Roosevelt's final message had some effect, therefore, in bringing about the resumption of negotiations. As Chamberlain started for Munich, profound relief was expressed in the United States, which wanted any issue of the controversy that would avert war.

At the height of the crisis the whole Western world had been convulsed. Capital moved in headlong flight from London, Paris, and other centers to New York, throwing foreign exchange into confusion. Sterling gyrated wildly. Great quantities of gold were bought in western Europe for shipment to the United States. Shipping insurance soared skyward. While the European and American stock markets registered spectacular declines, farmers of the Middle West and stockmen of the plains witnessed a sharp drop in all primary commodities. Thousands of American tourists and businessmen abroad, warned by black headlines and by diplomatic officials, were racing for homeward ports.

The *Europa* of the North German Lloyd, setting out for America with eleven hundred paassengers, was suddenly recalled on the 28th while in the English Channel. Other German ships were ordered to head for the nearest neutral haven. Since the whole world believed that fighting was at hand, proportionately great was its joy when, on September 30, Hitler, Mussolini, Chamberlain, and Daladier signed an agreement pledging peace at the cost of giving the Nazis nearly a free hand in the Sudetenland.

"I believe it is peace in our time," said Chamberlain—and many Germans hoped so with him. When just after the conference Chamberlain drove about Munich, the crowds cheered him with hearty demonstration of gratitude. He laid before Hitler a pledge of mutual consultation on all problems affecting European peace, and Hitler signed it with frigid demeanor—and every intention of breaking it. Although the Fuehrer said in a speech that since the new settlement "Germany has no more territorial problems in Europe," he immediately asked General Keitel to give him data upon the military forces required to break down all Czech resistance.

We now know that within a fortnight Keitel gave his answer. We know that hardly a month had elapsed after Munich when Hitler issued to the leaders of the armed forces a directive which defined their future task: "Liquidation of the remainder of Czechoslovakia." But the world's relief was far from implying any approval of the Munich terms, which pared away Czechoslovakia's boundaries, left the little country practically defenseless, and at one stroke canceled forty divisions of troops. Relief and humiliation constituted the Anglo-French mood. Relief and disgust represented the American mood. Secretary Hull struck a warning note. "I am not undertaking to pass upon the merits of the differences to which the Four-Power Pact signed at Munich on yesterday related," he said. He urged the forces of peace not to relax, but to redouble their efforts to maintain the principles of order under law. On November 1 he told the American people that the world was moving along a road which led to catastrophe, and that unless the nations took a sharp turn, they would soon be engulfed in a new world war, "the horror and destructiveness of which will pass human imagination."

Munich was a great turning point in world history. Britain and France gradually saw that it represented a profound miscalculation. The Chamberlain-Bonnet policy of appeasement had been founded on the false idea that just as Bismarck had halted German expansion and turned toward peace once the unification of Germany had been achieved in the Franco-Prussian war, so Hitler

would now be ready to stop short. The fact was
that Hitler could not stop. The basic Nazi aim
was the establishment of the Reich as a power
possessing complete freedom of action, self-
sufficient in the ownership of Ukrainian minerals,
Caucasian oil, Hungarian grain, and Belgian steel;
to turn back before this was won would be to
destroy the Nazi movement. Britain at last realized
this grim impossibility of compromise. The Western democracies had lost much by Munich. They
had lost the forty Czech divisions, the great arsenal of Czech munitions plants, and most of their
moral prestige in eastern Europe. They had
gained a year of time—the year in which the Royal
Air Force was provided with the Spitfire and Hur-
ricane that finally won the Battle of Britain.

As for the Americans, the crisis had done much
to educate them to the realities of the international situation. Many still clung to the belief
that the United States could be general moral
inspector of the globe without assuming any responsibilities. Now they began to see that the
world was shrinking fast in size, and that their
own fate was inextricably interwoven with that of
other peoples. Nor was this all; for the whole
climate of world affairs had suddenly changed.
Hitherto the augmentation of Germany's power
had been regarded as the affair of Europe alone;
now men saw that it might become a very serious

threat to the New World. The sharp decline in British prestige was a sobering event. It had been the authority of Britain in Europe, and the strength of the British navy on the seas, which had given the United States during most of the nineteenth century a happy sense of freedom from Old World complications. Britain had stood as guarantor that no great power would break out upon the North Atlantic, and now that guaranty was suddenly swept away. The revelation of British and French weakness served notice that the United States must be on its guard.

By this time the United States had a new measure of public opinion in the Gallup, *Fortune*, and other polls. Just before Munich, Mr. Gallup's Institute of Public Opinion questioned representative elements on their willingness, if war began in Europe, to sell food and war materials to Britain and France. Only 57 per cent favored selling food; only 34 per cent selling war materials. Not long after Munich the same poll was taken again. This time 82 per cent favored selling food, and 57 per cent war munitions. No fewer than 62 per cent said that the totalitarian powers would be an immediate menace to the United States if they won. More and more Americans saw that it was necessarily to arm speedily, to do everything practicable to sustain Britain and France, and to consider future world contingencies with care. The position of the United States in Latin America, the Far East, and Europe had to be reviewed with attention to the possibility of an attack on both flanks by massively armed and utterly ruthless nations.

The striking down of Austria and Czechoslovakia resulted in a shocking accentuation of a problem in which many Americans felt keen concern—that of the refugees. Hitler, trying to weld a strong national feeling in Germany and to make an effective appeal to the baser elements, had promoted race prejudice. He had caught up the myth of a Nordic race as the chosen seed of an original Aryan race. Nothing but mysticism could tolerate such a perniciously erroneous concept, for Europe had no pure race, and the Germans were even more weirdly mixed than most surrounding peoples. Yet the new generation turned credulously to Rosenberg's *Myth of the Twentieth Century* and Hitler's *Mein Kampf*, with their volent attacks upon "inferior" races, among whom the Jews were foremost. Determined to make Germany intolerable to all Jews, the Nazi regime had pursued with increasing vigor its policy of confiscating Jewish property, driving Jews out of business and the professions, and destroying their cultural institutions. By 1938, no fewer than 130,000 Jews had abandoned the Reich. Year by year, despite restrictions on immigration, a steady seepage came into American ports. Those

who remained within the Reich, comprising many
aged and ailing as well as a stubborn body determined to fight for their rights, suffered a ceaseless
persecution.

As the problem grew, governmental action became imperative, and the United States was clearly
the country to take the lead. It had the largest
resources; more and more of the refugees were
coming to it; and its influence was strongest. In
March, 1938, Hull, who was deeply moved, asked
various nations of Europe and Latin America to
establish a committee to assist in refugee emigration from Austria and Germany. The money would
be supplied from private sources and no country
would be asked to relax its existing immigration
quotas (the United States certainly did not wish
to do so). A little later Roosevelt told the press
that the committee would look after refugees from
all countries: from Soviet Russia, Spain, and Italy
as well as Central Europe. All the Governments
approached accepted the invitation save Italy,
which declined because it could hardly succor Hitler's victims while swearing eternal friendship to
Hitler himself. A conference was arranged at Evian-
les-Bains in France, where on July 6, 1938, delegates gathered from thirty-two nations, electing
Myron C. Taylor, a leading American industrialist,
their president.

The conference set up an Intergovernmental

Committee on political refugees, which forthwith established headquarters in London and prepared to negotiate with the Reich Government on improved conditions of emigration. The chairman was an American, George Rublee. All the nations at Evian had been generous in sympathy but guarded in offers of anything more substantial. The United States, tormented by mass unemployment, was averse to throwing its gates wide open. Canada also pleaded economic reasons for refusing newcomers. France declared that, having already absorbed more than 200,000 refugees, she had reached the extreme saturation limit. Australia, Brazil, and Argentina, lands with vast open spaces, declared against a more generous immigration policy, for all feared economic or social difficulties. Those few nations which showed any disposition to accept large numbers, notably Colombia, Mexico, and Peru, wanted agricultural labor—and most of Hitler's victims were people of urban habits.

A series of events during 1938 made the situation steadily worse. As soon as the swastika flag flew over Austria, a club descended on the heads of Jews and liberals. Flight offered the only safety. But neighboring countries closed their borders, lest they offend the Fuehrer. Italy, repudiating her long record of tolerance, resorted to a policy of expulsion and repression. This angered Americans. Talk of a boycott of Italian goods sprang up in

New York, and Justice Costillo, in the name of the millions of Italian origin living in the United States, vainly appealed to the Duce to moderate his decrees. Next month Poland manifested even greater cruelty. The Germans had been deporting many Polish Jews. Warsaw suddenly issued orders under which no holder of a Polish passport granted outside the country could, after October 30, return without special permission. The Germans at once speeded up their deportations, gathering together about 30,000 Poles in the single night of October 27, and pushing them aboard trains; and the Polish Government retaliated by arresting many Germans and preparing to dump them into the Reich.

Then in November came a climactic event. A young Polish Jew who had fled to Paris made his way into the German Embassy and fatally shot the first official he found. The controlled Nazi press broke into frenzied incitements to violence. Mobs, encouraged by Nazi officials, roamed the cities seizing, beating, and torturing helpless Jews. Synagogues were burned, shops were wrecked, houses were plundered. The police, far from interfering, arrested thousands of inoffensive Jews of both sexes and all ages, herding them into prisons and concentration camps. A fine of a billion marks ($420,-000,000) was imposed on the Jews of the Reich as a penalty for the murder. And in the wake of this

cold-blooded, government-fostered pogrom, a flock
of new laws and decrees made the lot of the
Jewish people worse than ever. It was evident
overnight that a mass exodus from Germany was
inevitable.

Coming immediately after Munich, these events
tore the last veils from Germany's character and
purpose. Roosevelt struck the keynote of popular
feeling when he ordered the American Ambassador
in Berlin home—permanently—for report and consultation.

The same chords of angry horror vibrated
throughout other English-speaking nations: in
Canada, Australia, and the British Isles. The last
vestiges of the old doctrine of appeasement were
being torn up in Great Britain, so that, when the
final obliteration of Czechoslovakia came, the idea
was held in loathing. In the United States the feeling that Nazi Germany was a monster whose aggressions must be opposed by all civilized nations
gave isolationism a heavy blow. The Jewish com-
munity naturally spurned the isolationist creed
and was for helping any nation which would fight
Germany. Many Catholics, deeply stirred by
Hitler's open enmity to their Church, felt the same
emotion. They remembered that the previous
October the Pope, sending a message to a Eucha-
ristic Congress in New Orleans, had delivered himself with unwonted emphasis. "Scarcely can we

refrain from tears," he wrote, "when we behold the eternal majesty of God Himself set aside and outraged, or with unspeakable wickedness held up, as an enemy, to reviling and execration."

The boycott of German goods had now spread throughout the United States. The press was filled with bitter comments on Nazi policies, Nazi leadership, and the few remaining American sympathizers with Nazism. Just before Christmas, Secretary Ickes, speaking in Cleveland, expressed a widely held sentiment when he attacked Henry Ford and Charles A. Lindbergh for taking the order of the German Eagle. The German Chargé d'Affaires, under instructions from Berlin, went to the State Department to demand an official expression of regret. He got instead an unforgettable reproof as Sumner Welles, Acting Secretary of State, brusquely rejected the protest.

Meanwhile, increasing anxiety was created in the United States by the incessant and virulent propaganda of Germany and Italy in South America. Both nations had sent large bodies of emigrants to the areas south of Panama. Both had from the beginning met some success in exporting Fascist ideas there. The concept of dictatorship was familiar to Latin Americans, and to many seemed a more natural and effective instrument of government than the Anglo-Saxon principle of representative democratic government based on the principle of compromise between parties. Revolutions had been common in South America, and had usually terminated in the personal rule of some strong figure, a Diaz, Machado, or Castro. The want of a strong middle class, of broadly diffused education, and of basic traditions of popular self-government, made the southern continent fertile ground for the ideas of Hitler and Mussolini. These ideas, to be sure, needed sharp modification in Latin America, where totalitarianism in the German sense was unknown, where the forms of government were republican, and where considerable freedom of the press and public assemblage was permitted. Still, a modified Fascism could easily become a menace—and it could offer New World partnerships to Hitler and Mussolini.

In Argentina and Chile, which had large populations of German blood, vigorous Nazi organizations came into existence. The gray-shirted Nacistas of Chile actually launched an unsuccessful revolt in Santiago in the early fall of 1938. On its failure their leaders turned about-face to join a coalition of Leftist parties called the Popular Front, which carried the October elections and chose Aguirre Cerda as President of the republic. Across the border in Argentina more than 40,000 persons had enrolled in Nazi units before the end of 1938, and their number was increasing. German schools had become numerous, and resounded with cries of "Heil Hitler!" When it was complained that they taught alien ideals instead of Argentine patriotism, the Government closed a number of them. Finally, in the spring of 1939, the Argentine regime outlawed the Nazi party, which had been charged with plotting to deliver Patagonia to the Reich. At the same time the Chileans gathered up an obnoxious German propagandist and deported him.

But it was in Brazil that the Germans and Italians succeeded in creating the greatest disturbance. Their strength in Santa Catharina and Rio Grande do Sul was almost sufficient to control those two great states. A Fascist party, the Integralists, sprang up with the usual paraphernalia of shirts, banners, and salutes, and with special doctrines—anti-Semitism, anti-Communism, and a clamorous nationalism. German and Italian radio stations, traveling lecturers, books, and pamphlets helped to nurture the new cult. Because Germany bought large quantities of Brazilian coffee and cotton, and because the German settlers had been notably thrifty and progressive, the Reich exercised a large influence upon the economic life of the country. German schools in some areas completely monopolized education and helped perpetuate an almost purely German culture. In Rio Grande do Sul more than 2,800 existed at the beginning of 1938, and only a score of them gave instruction in the Portuguese language. When at the end of 1937 President Getulio Vargas gave himself by a bold *coup d'état* six more years of power, he dissolved the Integralists as a political party. They promptly went underground, and early the next year Government officials found them plotting a revolution and the assassination of the President. Large quantities of arms and munitions were uncovered. The result was a series of sharp repressive measures.

Everywhere, from Mexico to the Strait of Magellan, the totalitarian states seemed to be making trouble. They were marshaling and indoctrinating people of German and Italian blood, intriguing against the rightful governments, and watching their chance to deliver some bold stroke. They were establishing newspapers, shipping facilities, and air lines—Germans by 1940 operated more than 10,000 miles of air routes in half a dozen countries. They were placing chosen agents in positions of power; they were ready to turn southern Brazil into a Nazi stronghold; they were plotting incessantly against Great Britain and the United States. They looked upon the Japanese colonists in Brazil as natural allies. It was clear to Washington that when the moment was ripe they would strike —and strike hard. With ambitious Latin-American politicians ready to serve them, they might actually plunge parts of Latin America into civil war. Should the Germans, Nazis, and Japanese ever seize control of Europe, their multitudinous agents in the New World would become a grave threat to American democracy. Germany might gain a foothold in western Africa—and then eastern Brazil would be but a short distance by air or sea from their striking power.

Not the Government alone, but the American people, saw in these efforts at the political and economic penetration of South America a serious menace. They were but partially reassured by the success of the Pan-American Conference at Lima in December, 1938. As we have seen, it issued a "Declaration of American Principles," while more importantly, it drew up a "Declaration of the Solidarity of America," under which the republics declared that they would maintain their sovereignty against all intervention, and would act in unison whenever the peace, security, or territorial integrity of any American republic should be threatened. The conference agreed that the Foreign Ministers of the various republics should hold a meeting the moment any critical situation arose.

The world's burden of armaments was now becoming almost insupportable. Germany and Russia were throwing the greater part of their national resources into the effort to arm to the teeth; Britain and France were frantically trying to regain lost ground; and the United States had perforce to join in the race. The appropriations of the great powers far outstripped those which had left thoughtful men aghast just before the catastrophe of 1914. Conservative estimates place the sums spent at twelve billions of dollars in 1937, and fifteen billions in 1938; one careful student even puts the total at fifteen and a half billions in 1937 and more than seventeen and a half billions in 1938.

The three aggressive powers, Germany, Italy, and Japan, and the four strong powers standing on the defensive, America, Britain, France, and Russia, were far and away the leaders in the armament race. All were straining their economies in the contest. Not one of these nations by 1938 could balance its budget. Russia and Japan that year were supposed to be putting two-fifths of their national income into guns; Germany one-sixth; France one-seventh; and even Britain one-four-teenth.

The United States was arming fast—and arming, plainly, against Germany, Italy, and Japan. It was impossible to say whether Japan might attack first, or Germany and Italy might deal the initial blow; whether Russia in the east, or France and Britain in the west, would feel the initial weight of the onslaught; whether America would be drawn into the conflict immediately, or after a year or two of waiting. What was certain was that war was plainly imminent in the world.

When Congress met in January, 1938, Roosevelt sent it a budget message in which he asked $957,000,000 for defense purposes during the fiscal year ending June 30, 1938, and $991,000,000 during the fiscal year ending June 30, 1939. The request was well received. But he had hardly made it before the Administration concluded that the sums were not large enough. Three weeks later, on January 28, Roosevelt sent a second message, asking that the existing naval authorizations be augmented by 20 per cent. Two battleships were under construction; two more were included in a naval appropriation bill which had just passed the House and was coming before the Senate; and now he requested two others, making six in all. The United States was to have a navy second to none; indeed, a navy greater than any other. Why? "As commander-in-chief of the Army and Navy," stated Roosevelt, "it is my constitutional duty to report to Congress that our national defense is, in the light of increasing armaments of other nations, inadequate for the purposes of national security and requires increase for that reason."

Pacifists and isolationists took the view that the existing armaments of the United States were quite adequate for defense, that the Administration must be covertly laying plans for offensive operations, and that these probably involved cooperation with Great Britain and perhaps other powers. Possibly, such men as Hiram Johnson suggested, secret commitments had already been made. Because a Navy Department divisional chief visited London to confer there on the question whether Britain, France, and the United States should not make a joint request for information on Japan's building plans, Johnson filled the Senate with sinister hints. He introduced a resolution demanding whether "any alliance, agreement, or understanding exists or is contemplated with Great Britain relating to war or the possibility of war"; whether there was any express or implied understanding for the use of the navy "in conjunction with any other nation"; and whether any agreement existed for the employment of our navy in patrolling "any particular waters." Secretary Hull promptly wrote a letter to the Chairman of the Foreign Relations Committee repeating each of these questions, and responding bluntly to every one: "The answer is 'No.'"

The appropriation for the naval increases passed. So did other defense appropriations. The nation was not willing to take any chances. As it watched the grim march of events in Europe and Asia, as it saw the manifest weakness of Britain and France, as crowds of pitiful refugees streamed into American ports, as news came of the unrelenting psychological assault upon Latin America, and as the plain citizen found himself compelled to accept unprecedented taxation for national defense, the mood of the country grew grimmer. Its illusions were fast melting away.

CHAPTER VII

THE EUROPEAN CATACLYSM BEGINS

TILL the very eve of the outbreak of war in Europe the fundamental schism in American foreign policy continued. The great object of the President was to bring moral pressure to bear against the aggressors, to encourage resistance in the countries menaced by them, and to effect a repeal of the Neutrality Act with its dangerous promise of a hands-off attitude by the United States in any future war. The great object of the Congressional majority was to keep the United States rigidly aloof from the Old World. The President had to emphasize the danger of war and the improbability of long-continued American exemption from it. Congressional isolationists derided the idea, and insisted that even if war began America could fence it out. The effect of this quarrel was to confuse public opinion and paralyze American action. More than once the President was compelled to halt and draw back for fear of an explosion of hostile feeling in Congress.

As 1939 opened, Roosevelt seized upon the annual Presidential message as a means of renewing his warnings. "All about us," he said, "rage undeclared wars—military and economic." (He did not mention that the United States had played its full part in the economic warfare.) The march of despotism and violence, he went on, constituted an assault upon democracy, international justice, and religion, and the defense of these threatened institutions was a general duty. "God-fearing democracies of the world which observe the sanctity of treaties and good faith in their dealings with other nations cannot safely be indifferent to international lawlessness anywhere. They cannot forever let pass, without effective protest, acts of aggression against sister nations—acts which automatically undermine all of us." What effective protest was possible without war? The President's answer was not convincing: "There are many methods short of war . . . of bringing home to aggressor governments the aggregate sentiments of our own people." Presumably he had in mind an economic embargo. But when he recommended a modification of those neutrality laws which "may actually give aid to an aggressor and deny it to the victim," he knew that a Congressional majority was still adamant against this elementary step.

After Munich, Government policy in Britain and France, with public sentiment in tremendous force behind it, rapidly shifted from appeasement to resistance. Chamberlain assured a Birmingham audience on January 28, 1939, that any attempt to dominate the world by force would be a challenge which "the democracies would inevitably resist." When Hitler told the Reichstag two days later that the riches of the world must be divided equitably or else "divided by force," and that the eighty million Germans living on limited resources must "export or die," the British and French Governments responded defiantly. Chamberlain announced that "any threat to the vital interests of France, from whatever quarter it came, must evoke the immediate cooperation of this country." A White Paper on rearmament showed that the British were increasing their expenditures for defense at a tremendous pace, the whole amount allotted for the purpose in 1936–42 exceeding two billion pounds. At the same time the British were not unwilling to make concessions to Germany in colonial and commercial spheres. Anxious to see the German economy transferred from a martial to a peaceful basis, they sent F. T. Ashton-Gwatkin to Berlin to lay the foundations for a trade agreement.

But it was too late for either a show of resistance or a promise of economic benefits to stop Hitler. Determined to take over the remnant of Czechoslovakia, he brushed aside the French and British request that he make good his promised guarantee of her frontiers. Germany could not join in an international pledge, he stated, until the Czechs met a long list of conditions. Goering later testified (Nuremberg, March 14, 1946) that he had opposed the conquest of Czechoslovakia, saying that this might be the straw that would break the back of the Chamberlain Government in Britain and bring Winston Churchill into power. To be sure, Czechoslovakia was looking to Moscow, but he argued that this would mean little, since the country would have to depend increasingly on Germany in an economic sense. Hitler, however, had received information that Russian aviators were training in Czechoslovakia, and believed the nation was about to become a nest of Soviet air bases threatening Germany. The internal weaknesses of Czechoslovakia, where a separatist movement of Slovaks and Ruthenians had become formidable, gave the German Government its opportunity. On March 6, President Hacha had to proclaim martial law in many towns; on March 13, Joseph Tiso, the Slovak leader, flew to Berlin; and on March 14, the Slovakian Diet voted by a heavy majority in favor of independence. German troops immediately occupied Prague and other centers and, on March 16, Hitler proclaimed a German protectorate over Bohemia and Moravia.

This was a flagrant repudiation of the Munich

agreement; it was clear notice to the world that nothing but superior force would stop Hitler. The last illusions of pacifists in Britain and France were destroyed. From this moment it was plain that a new world conflict could be averted only by a miracle.

The American Government refused to recognize the new regime. Sumner Welles, Acting Secretary of State, lost no time in condemning the "temporary extinguishment of the liberties of a free and independent people." Within a week, Hitler's forces seized the long-disputed district of Memel from Lithuania. Proposals were simultaneously presented to Warsaw for the German annexation of Danzig and of a territorial strip bridging the Polish Corridor. The world steeled itself for a blow against Poland. Instead, the next act of aggression took place in Albania. Mussolini, who had long coveted that little principality, threw troops across the Adriatic (April 7), and after a few days of almost bloodless marching, established his mastery. Once more the State Department spoke its mind plainly, Secretary Hull attacking this "forcible and violent invasion" as a new menace to world peace.

London and Paris felt their backs against the wall. The Czechoslovakian bastion, with its forty divisions, had melted away. If Poland were destroyed, the Nazis would so dominate Europe that their word would be law from the Carpathians to the Channel. On the morrow of Czechoslovakia's extinction, March 16, Chamberlain again addressed a Birmingham audience. Hitler's action, he declared, was a violation of his promises before, during, and after the Munich settlement. How could anyone take his word for the future? The dictators might try to conquer all Europe. "No greater mistake could be made than to suppose that . . . this nation has so lost its fibre that it will not take part to the utmost of its power in resisting such a challenge if it were ever made."

Two days later, on March 18, Daladier asked the French Chamber to give his Government dictatorial authority until the end of November, and the Deputies at once did so. Great Britain and France were working in close unison, asserted Daladier; and his Ministry would not yield to force or intrigue "a single one of our rights or an acre of our territory." An immediate state visit by President Lebrun to London underlined the fact of the Anglo-French alliance. The exchanges between Germany and Poland on the Danzig question were closely watched. When Warsaw in effect defied Von Ribbentrop and a deadlock ensued, Anglo-French fears of some sudden assault mounted. London and Paris resolved to join in a firm guarantee of Polish independence. Speaking in the House on March 31, Chamberlain sounded a note of clarion timbre. If any action occurred "which clearly threatened Polish independence, and which the Polish Government accordingly considered it vital to resist with their national forces, His Majesty's Government would consider themselves bound at once to lend the Polish Government all support in their power."

The day after Chamberlain's speech, while its echoes were ringing around the world, Hitler addressed a crowd gathered to watch the launching of the Reich's second 35,000-ton battleship, the *Admiral Von Tirpitz.* He denounced Great Britain, and declared that from that date the Anglo-German naval agreement was a dead letter.

During the first week of April, the Polish Foreign Minister, Joseph Beck, was in London. A series of conferences took place. At their close, Chamberlain announced that a permanent reciprocal agreement would bind Great Britain and Poland, the two nations standing pledged to fly to each other's assistance "in the event of any threat, direct or indirect, to the independence of either." This compact, he explained, implied no aggressive intent. Immediately thereafter, both Britain and France extended their guarantees to cover Rumania and Greece on the simple condition that if they were driven to defend their independence against aggression by armed force, they would then be entitled to all the support the two powers could muster.

Turkey had received credits from both Germany and Britain, but she well understood which would be the safer partner. In the middle of May an agreement was announced by which the British and Turks were to give each other assistance if any aggressive act led to war in the Mediterranean area. By this time, the British Government had sent Parliament a budget of well over six billion dollars, of which about half was for war purposes; had announced the forthcoming creation of a Ministry of Supplies; and was placing the Territorial forces, now increased to 340,000 men, upon a war footing.

The new Anglo-French measures greatly pleased Roosevelt and the two other men most responsible for American foreign policy, Secretaries Hull and Morgenthau. The formation of the "peace front" seemed to them emphatically the correct course. Already the British had let contracts for a large number of airplanes to be built in America. The French, ready to do the same, were anxious to obtain the most efficient models. When a French mission started for the United States, Ambassador Bullitt requested that it be allowed to see some of the latest types of army and navy planes. To Roosevelt and Morgenthau this seemed highly proper. When Secretary of War Woodring, an inveterate isolationist, placed obstacles in the path, he was brusquely by-passed. Morgenthau was given a clear field by the President and used his powers with adroitness and dispatch. Every effort was made to avoid publicity; but when a new Douglas bomber crashed in California with a French observer inside, headlines blazed throughout the country. Plainly, the Government had lent France a hand in preparing against Germany.

The sequel was a hearing of the Senate Military Affairs Committee at which Morgenthau explained to isolationists Nye and Bennett Champ Clark that no law or Federal regulation had been violated, and that foreign contracts were invaluable in vitalizing our dangerously weak airplane industry. The committee called on the President, who offered further explanations. So nervous was Roosevelt over the possibility that isolationist groups might create an agitation damaging to his main objects that the fact that he had signed a paper authorizing Morgenthau's action was suppressed. But he spoke bluntly to the Senators. Though the meeting was supposedly secret, they let the press know that he had said, in effect: "America's first line of defense is in France." This elementary truth caused an uproar. Roosevelt had long since learned, as a practiced yachtsman, to make progress by a series of tacks. His bold statement was a contribution to the education of the public in unwelcome realities; but he at once allayed the shock by declaring that the report was a "deliberate lie," and by making a milder statement to his press conference of February 3. In this he said that his policy covered four main points:

1. No entangling alliances.
2. Maintenance of full world trade.
3. Support of every effort at armament reduction.
4. As a nation—as the American people—we are sympathetic with the peaceful maintenance of political, economic, and social independence of all nations in the world.

Having thus veered, the President at once stood on a straight course again. Leaving Warm Springs after a brief vacation on April 9, he remarked to the press: "I'll be back in the fall if we don't have a war." Three days later he astonished the world by announcing that he had sent a personal message asking Hitler and Mussolini to make their intentions clear in a fashion which would give the small nations of Europe and Asia assurance of their future safety.

If the President's object was to delay a blow by Hitler at Danzig—which many observers believed had been prepared for the last ten days of April— it was successful. If the object was to place the two dictators on the defensive and extort pledges which might tie their hands for the future, it was a complete failure. Neither sent a written reply. Both prepared public responses. Roosevelt, after listing the countries which had recently lost their independence, had named twenty-one other lands which might fear aggression, and had asked if the two leaders were "willing to give assurances that your armed forces will not attack or invade" these nations. Specifically, he proposed a non-aggression pledge for ten years, to be made reciprocal by the countries covered.

Mussolini adopted an attitude of outraged innocence. Speaking on April 20 at Rome, he disclaimed any intention of attacking another country and accused Roosevelt of a colossal ignorance of European affairs. Hitler thought of the ingenious trick of querying various small countries as to their fear of German attack—receiving, of course, the politic reply from most of them that they confided in the good faith of the Reich and every other power! Rumania alone had the courage to express apprehensions. Hitler then, on April 28, delivered a clever address to the Reichstag, concluding with a declaration that the German Government would give each state named such an assurance as Roosevelt had asked, on condition of absolute reciprocity, if the state sent in a request accompanied by "correspondingly acceptable proposals."

This plainly held the door wide to aggression, for Poland would never make acceptable proposals. As if to leave no doubt of his intentions, Hitler used the speech to announce a formal abrogation of the naval agreement with Great Britain, and of the Non-Aggression Treaty which Germany and Poland had concluded in 1934. The excuse he gave was the antagonistic attitude of Great Britain, the Polish rejection of the "concrete offer" made to Warsaw, and the new compact of Britain and Poland for mutual aid. Mussolini at once placed himself at Hitler's side. With much fanfare, Foreign Minister Ciano met Von Ribbentrop at Milan on May 6–7, where they agreed to a military pact; and Ciano shortly proceeded to Berlin for its formal signature. Each power bound itself unequivocally to go to the aid of the other "with all its military forces on land, sea, and in the air" in the event that hostilities began. Measures were at once taken to bring the air forces and secret police of the two nations into close relations, and to lay plans for unifying their economies— measures that seemed to look toward an early war.

Instead of placing the dictatorships on the defensive, Roosevelt's letter had given them an opportunity to delude their people by more talk about "encirclement." The President had done his best, but Hitler and Mussolini were not influenced by American words. If they thought about transatlantic affairs at all, they took encouragement from Congressional opponents of the Chief Executive. We now know that on May 23, Hitler announced to a secret council at the Reich Chancellery in Berlin that he would, for certain reasons which he then gave, attack Poland at the first good opportunity.

Roosevelt and Hull had means of knowing that war in Europe was imminent. The American people had not. As the fatal hour drew nearer, it was more and more important that the rigid arms embargo against all belligerents be lifted. The President was aware that Congress, with his initial acquiescence, had deprived him of his strongest weapon against the dictators. If Hitler attacked Poland, Britain, and France, Roosevelt and Hull might be inclined to send aid to the Western democracies, but they would be helpless; they might be interventionists, but the law would remain isolationist.

The President acted through the heads of the Senate and House Committees on Foreign Affairs to bring heavy pressure upon members of Congress. To numerous Senators he talked at length. War might well begin within the year, he remarked, and a general European conflict would seriously threaten the safety of the United States. To these warnings, reiterated throughout the spring of 1939, most Congressional leaders remained deaf. They believed that the European powers would not dare go to war, and that, even if they did, the United States could keep aloof.

The isolationists suspected the President and State Department; they feared a return to Wilsonian policies. The Administration had its Congressional adherents draft a bill for repeal of the embargo, but it was clearly doomed to defeat. On July 11, 1939, the Senate committee voted 12 to 11 against reporting it.

In a final effort to influence the obdurate Senate leaders, Roosevelt called a group to meet him and Hull at the White House. The President opened the conference with a solemn warning. It might be well to begin with prayer, he said, for the decisions about to be taken would influence the whole world. Once more he pointed to the imminent danger of war, the encouragement which the totalitarian powers would extract from the arms embargo in preparing a conflict, and the need for democratic solidarity. One Senator inquired if it was possible that war might begin before Congress met again in January, 1940; he responded that it was. Hull delivered a fervent exhortation to the Senators, pleading earnestly and even emotionally. Senator Borah, however, as spokesman for the isolationist phalanx, remained skeptical. Vice-President Garner, who had attempted to bring Senators into line, asked each man present if he believed that enough votes could be obtained for a repeal. The unanimous verdict was that defeat was certain. Garner summed up the decision: "Well, Captain," he told

Roosevelt with a smile, "you haven't got the votes."

Throughout the late spring and summer the British and French had been laboring to bring the Russian Government into a defensive combination against Germany. So long as Maxim Litvinov was in charge of foreign affairs in Moscow, the prospect that the Soviet Union would continue to oppose German aggrandizement was good. Even after Litvinov fell from power on May 3 and was replaced by Vyacheslav Molotov, who took an attitude of hostile suspicion toward the Western democracies, it still seemed probable that Russian policy would remain unaltered.

But sharp difficulties arose. The Russians remembered Munich, and Molotov had expressed the deduction they drew from that affair when he warned the people on March 31 to bear in mind "Stalin's precept to be cautious and not to allow our country to be drawn into conflicts by warmongers who are accustomed to have others pull the chestnuts out of the fire for them." The British and French remembered Russia's desertion of the front in 1918 and the long-continued troublemaking by the Comintern. But the chief obstacle to agreement was presented by the Baltic States and Poland. Russia wished an alliance with them and Rumania which would guarantee the independence of all the signatories, and insisted that, if they would not join the defensive combination, they should give facilities to Russian forces in time of war. So, also, should Finland. But the Balts and Poles felt that any arrangement which permitted their soil to be occupied by Russian "protectors" was equivalent to a lamb's acceptance of protection by a hungry lion. The Poles would listen to no such proposal.

Hull was being steadily warned by American Embassies in Europe of Germany's preparations for war. As such warnings thickened, the Russian Government in a sudden nightmare change of front shifted to Germany's side, and threw open the gates for Hitler's attack on civilization. If Munich had been appeasement of aggressors, this was partnership with them. On August 15, an official in the German Foreign Office hinted to the British Ambassador in Berlin that Russia would shortly join in a new partition of Poland. On the 19th a trade and credit agreement between Russia and the Reich was suddenly announced. On the 23rd, Russia and Germany signed in Moscow a non-aggression pact in which they mutually agreed to withhold support from any nation which might go to war with either of them, and to keep aloof from any group of powers formed to check either. This was a diplomatic revolution. The Soviet Union had been expected to support peace by impeding Nazi aggression; instead, it supported war by encouraging the gangsters now ready to march under the swastika banner. The State Department was not taken wholly by surprise, for it had learned almost a year earlier that Germany had offered Russia such a pact as was now signed.

For this *volte-face*, Stalin and Molotov received their price. Part of it was the promise of Hitler's regime to drop the antagonism to Communism which had been one of the basic Nazi creeds. Part of it was the prospect that in a bloody European civil war, Germany, France, Poland, and Britain would soon be tearing each other into shreds, and thereby weakening the Continent in all its dealings with the Soviet Union. Part of it was more substantial: by a secret treaty annexed to the agreement, Russia was given the right to advance westward over the Baltic States and Poland to the line of the Narew, Vistula, and San rivers. It was in accordance with this secret treaty, not disclosed until after the war, that, as the Germans thrust deep into Poland, the Russians surged forward to meet them. Great Britain had been too scrupulous to force the Baltic States, Finland, and Poland to give the Soviet Union footholds; Russia now made ready to obliterate their independence. The immorality of the transaction astonished few people familiar with Kremlin tactics, but the dubious wisdom of the step aroused much wonder.

The springs of Russian foreign policy lay chiefly

in the dogmas of Marxist and Leninist thought, which led Moscow to believe that an unbridgeable gulf lay between its Communist regime and the capitalist world, and that a cynical opportunism was required in dealing with all Western powers. The Nazi-Soviet documents later published by the State Department, the Nuremberg documents, and other papers, indicate that as early as March 10 Stalin had determined to keep out of the impending war and to work with the Nazis; and that the initiative for the partnership now concluded actually came from the Soviet side. It was a nauseating story.

In America the effect of this Stalin-Hitler deal was tremendous. The *Nation* and *New Republic*, long friendly to Russia, denounced it without restraint. The Communist weekly *The New Masses* lost some of its best contributors, including Granville Hicks and Kyle Crichton. The Teachers' Union, which had been under Communist influence, ejected Jerome Davis from its presidency and elected George S. Counts, an anti-Communist, in his stead. A long list of writers who had usually shown cordiality toward the Russian experiment, headed by Heywood Broun and Louis Fischer, sharply turned to the right, forsook the fellow travelers, and assailed Russian policy as indefensible. On the other hand, liberals and Socialists who had for years declared that Moscow was not to be trusted found themselves vindicated by events. W. H. Chamberlin, who had covered Russia for the *Christian Science Monitor* and had been revolted by the ruthless treatment of the peasants; Benjamin Stolberg, an expert on labor; John Dewey, philosopher and educator; Max Eastman, author and Socialist leader—these were among the men whose warnings, as most people agreed, were now proved valid. Condemnation of the Moscow pact was general. But dismay preponderated over indignation, for a new world cataclysm was plainly at hand.

The German invasion of Poland at dawn on September 1 tragically fulfilled the prophecies made by Roosevelt and Hull in July. In 1914 American sentiment had been divided on responsibility for the European war; in World War II it placed full responsibility upon the Nazi leaders. Sympathy was overwhelmingly on the side of Britain and France. The President at once issued a Proclamation of Neutrality, but as he did so he told the country in a radio address that it must steel itself against heavy shocks which might touch its vital interests. "This nation will remain a neutral nation," he said, "but I cannot ask that every American remain neutral in thought as well. . . . Even a neutral cannot be asked to close his mind or conscience." In accordance with the Neutrality Act, Roosevelt had to forbid the exporta-

tion of arms, ammunition, and implements of war
to all the belligerents, including even Canada, the
nation's closest neighbor and most valued friend.
But he called Congress in special session on September 21, and went before it to demand repeal of
the embargo provisions.

Few of the President's state papers are more
interesting than the argument which he presented
for this long-overdue repeal. Only twice in its long
history under the Constitution, he stated, had the
United States deviated from a sound policy with
respect to neutral rights based on international
law. The first time was when in Jefferson's Administration it passed the Non-Intercourse and Embargo Acts. These laws completely failed to attain
their object. The second departure from principle
lay in the neutrality legislation of 1935–37, legislation which the President regretfully confessed
that he had failed to veto. These later enactments
had surrendered valuable American rights, including the historic principle of the freedom of neutrals
to navigate the high seas. But they had also affected the world situation in an unfortunate way.
They had placed the land powers on the same
footing as naval powers so far as commercial
privileges were concerned. "A land-power which
threatened war could thus feel assured in advance
that any prospective sea-power antagonist would

be weakened through denial of its ancient right to
buy anything anywhere."

Some opposition to Roosevelt's appeal appeared.
Not merely the familiar isolationist phalanx—
Borah, Nye, Hiram Johnson, David I. Walsh, and
the younger La Follette and Lodge—but some
more reasonable men were ready to vote "No."
Arthur H. Vandenberg of Michigan wished to preserve the embargo as "the all-controlling symbol
of an attitude." Public sentiment, however, had
emphatically expressed itself. A Gallup poll
showed that 62 per cent of the cross-section of
population questioned believed that the United
States should do everything possible to help Britain and France short of going to war; and 29 per
cent even held that, if Germany seemed about to
emerge victorious, the United States should enter
the conflict.

After a protracted floor battle, the President's
lieutenants carried the repeal to success. Prominent
among his aides was Senator James F. Byrnes of
South Carolina, who had polled many of his col-
leagues by long-distance telephone before Congress
met, and whose talents in persuasion were invaluable in Washington. Secretary Hull used all his
tremendous influence in both chambers. In the
House, the Democratic organization was almost
solidly aligned behind the President. The press was

overwhelmingly for repeal, and a long array of public bodies spoke with vigor on the subject. The new enactment revived and extended the old cash-and-carry clause (which had expired in May, 1939). This clause had applied only to raw materials useful in war; now it was expanded to include also munitions and manufactured military equipment. By a separate provision, the President was empowered to define combat zones from which all American ships were debarred. It was now possible for the Allies to buy a wide range of American stores and munitions as fast as they could provide ships to carry them.

Roosevelt's policy of aid for the democracies had its origin in the first month of the war, when he warmly urged Congress to repeal the arms embargo. From the date of the repeal aid was indeed one of the Government's main policies. But it had others, which under Roosevelt's bold leadership it pursued with a prevision and energy hardly paralleled in all its previous history. One part of the Administration's strategy in foreign affairs was to arm the nation as rapidly and expertly as possible. A second part was the consolidation of the republics of the New World in an unbreakable battalion to resist "the new philosophies of force" and to keep them from gaining a foothold in the Americas. The third part was to weaken the ag-

gressor powers in every way feasible, and to assist
the states which they were assailing. This at first
was done mainly by selling goods to Britain and
France, with the result that not far from half the
total exports of the United States (44.3 per cent)
in the first year of the conflict went to the British
Empire.

In defense, the most striking of the early rearmament steps concerned the navy. A "neutrality
patrol" was quickly instituted in Atlantic waters,
ostensibly to protect the American coasts in a
depth of 300 to 1,000 miles, and nominally with
the aid of other American republics. In reality this
aid was negligible, and no effort was made to keep
the warships of belligerents outside the wide patrol
zone. The main if not the only purpose served
was preparation for hostilities. First a few vessels
were used, then forty destroyers, then all the
destroyers and submarines that could be refitted.
Naval reservists were called into service; the enlist-
ment of sailors was increased. Admirable training
for war duties was given the crews, and ships were
tested under severe conditions. Meanwhile, a
naval expansion bill was debated in the fall of
1939. In its original form it provided for a 25 per
cent increase in the tonnage of all categories of
vessels below capital ships; it was shortly cut to an
11 per cent increase—but this permitted the addi-

tion of three carriers, eleven cruisers, and twenty-odd submarines to the navy. Naval aviation also received attention.

A fair degree of Hemispheric solidarity was meanwhile attained. The Latin republics wished to keep out of war; they wished American aid in keeping out; and they were glad to arrange for collective neutrality. The machinery for consultation provided at Buenos Aires and Lima was easily set in motion. Representatives of the twenty-one republics met at Panama City in what Under Secretary Sumner Welles correctly said was an unprecedented gathering. While intercontinental defense was the cardinal preoccupation, the delegates were also keenly interested in economic arrangements of a Hemispheric character which would do something to offset the anticipated collapse of European trade. German observers, including a minister who represented the Reich in the Central American states, were on hand. The opening address by the President of Panama made it clear that Latin America no less than English-speaking America was on the side of the Allies; but the general desire was to hold aloof from the Old World conflict. Sumner Welles spoke for all when he said that the republics would never submit that "their security, their nationals, or their legitimate commercial rights should be jeopardized by belligerent activities in close proximity to the shores of

the New World." He promised financial assistance
to the southern republics to meet the emergency
and set new industries on their feet, and men-
tioned a possible expansion of shipping services.

It was under the leadership of Welles that the
Panama Conference adopted its three principal
measures, one relating to a safety zone, one to a
united proclamation of neutrality, and one to the
creation of a committee to lighten the economic
impact of the war. These measures showed that
the machinery for consultation had genuine effec-
tiveness, and did something both to calm the nerves
of Latin America and to heighten the harmony
between the United States and its neighbors.

The establishment of a broad safety zone was a
gesture which, as we have indicated, did not effectively alter international law. Five million square
miles of ocean was too much for any navy to patrol. It was not long before the German pocket-
battleship *Graf Spee*, which was raiding commerce
in South American waters, was caught by three
British cruisers, the *Achilles*, *Ajax*, and *Exeter*, and
was forced into the harbor of Montevideo. Her
commander scuttled his ship and committed
suicide. Immediately thereafter a British cruiser
chased a German freighter into Fort Lauderdale,
Florida. Most Americans and Uruguayans did not
care how many German ships were pursued, sunk,
or captured in American waters.

The second measure, the issuance of a General
Declaration of Neutrality of the American Republics, was in the main a conventional step. The
twenty-one republics set forth the traditional
rights and duties of neutrals, adding that Governments might exclude submarines from their adjacent waters (as the United States wished to do),
or admit them under special regulations (as Argentina desired). An expert committee was set up
to give neutrality constant study. As for cushion-
ing the economic blows of the war, the prescription
of measures in this field was also entrusted to an
advisory committee, set up in Washington by the
Pan-American Union.

The "policy of aid for the democracies" of which
Roosevelt later spoke was meanwhile making
progress which by early spring of 1940 had reached
substantial proportions. It was a policy firmly
based, in a double sense, on self-interest: the
farther America could hold the German menace
from its own homes the better, and the more it
could use Anglo-French funds to build up its
weak airplane and munitions industries, the
stronger it would become. Even before the declaration of war, British contracts for airplanes had
reached a high figure. An Anglo-French Purchasing Mission shortly reached Washington, accompanied by technical experts. Establishing cordial
relations with Secretary Morgenthau, who was

deputed by the President to oversee the mission, the Anglo-French agents began letting contracts for small arms, ordnance, ammunition, and, most important of all, airplanes. Morgenthau's unwearied assistance was for several reasons of the first importance. He stood aloof from the bitter quarrel of Secretary Woodring and Assistant Secretary Louis Johnson in the Navy Department; he could take broader views of the program for national preparedness than either the War or Navy Departments; he supervised the expert Procurement Division of the Treasury, which constantly bought an immense variety of Government materials; and he was ardently devoted to the defense of democracy against the totalitarian states. With his assistance, help from Louis Johnson and Secretary of the Navy Edison, and the encouragement of President Roosevelt, a steady stream of materials soon flowed to Europe.

Throughout the winter of 1939–40, the period of dormant war in the West, the isolationists redoubled their efforts to persuade Americans that peace must be kept at any price. Even if Hitler won, they stubbornly insisted, the United States had nothing to fear. Indeed, whispered some, it might be well if divided Europe were at last molded into one peaceable unit by the strong Nazi grip; it might be well if America traded profitably with a rich and triumphant Germany. The leaders of this campaign were by now familiar figures. They included such veteran baiters of foreign lands as William Randolph Hearst, Col. Robert R. McCormick of the Chicago *Tribune*, and Patterson of the New York *Daily News;* such Western Senators as Burton K. Wheeler of Montana, Gerald P. Nye, and Robert M. La Follette, Jr.; the naive Hamilton Fish of New York, and the bigoted George H. Tinkham of Massachusetts; the aviator Charles A. Lindbergh, who inherited his father's views on world wars, and who was conscientious, unimaginative, and misled by crude ideas on the have and have-not nations; and various writers of minor renown. Among them were a curious sprinkling of specialists in international law. They were abetted by a German group under George Sylvester Viereck, later revealed as a Nazi agent with an ample treasure chest. A great deal of isolationist material went out under Congressional franks, and much of it had a pro-Nazi or anti-British tone.

Against these cohorts, however, an increasingly militant movement for peaceful support of the Allies was under way. In the autumn of 1939 a Non-Partisan Committee for Peace through revision of the Neutrality Law, frankly pro-Ally, sprang up. William Allen White became its head; such newspaper editors as Frank Knox of the Chicago *News,* Douglas Freeman of the Richmond

News-Leader, and Chester Rowell of the San Francisco *Chronicle* joined; presidents of numerous universities and colleges—Minnesota, North Carolina, Dartmouth, Smith—fell into line; so did religious leaders—Bishop Manning, President Henry S. Coffin of Union Theological Seminary, Msgr. John A. Ryan, and Rabbi Stephen S. Wise; and such noted writers as Dorothy Canfield Fisher, Ida M. Tarbell, and Robert Sherwood. A number of businessmen, such as Marshall Field of Chicago, enlisted. By the end of October, the Non-Partisan Committee was represented in thirty states, and a New York group inspired by Wendell Willkie was raising money to carry on its work. It gave invaluable help, by efficient publicity and White's energetic lobbying in Washington, to the revision of the neutrality legislation. Then in April, 1940, when the Germans suddenly invaded Denmark and Norway and the Nazi peril to the United States became intensified, White and Clark Eichelberger (director of the League of Nations Association) organized a new body to which White gave an inspired name: the Committee to Defend America by Aiding the Allies. In the work which it at once launched to educate the people and influence Congress, White was assisted by a lengthening roster of distinguished men. Among them were President Butler of Columbia University, Thomas W. Lamont, Frank L. Polk, former Under Secretary of State, and Colonel Henry L. Stimson. Month by month the internationalist press, led by the New York *Times* and *Herald Tribune*, spoke with greater insistence.

But events, not words, are the greatest educator. The smashing of Poland by the war machines of Germany and Russia and the brutal harrying of Finland by Soviet armies appalled reflective Americans. When two Scandinavian lands, closely linked with America by their immigrant sons and kinship of ideals, were crushed beneath the Nazi juggernaut, the lesson was written in fire on a blackened sky.

With the invasion of Denmark and Norway came a hurried enlargement of the Anglo-French purchasing program. Secretary Morgenthau's staff, acting with the British and French, had made the necessary arrangements. It was agreed that the American Government should release the latest-model planes, for example, on condition that the Allies pay part of the expenses of research and development. The very day after Washington heard of the lightning advance into Scandinavia, a large number of new contracts was signed, tentatively establishing a fresh program for the delivery of 2,440 fighters and 2,160 bombers. More munitions and war materials of every sort were hastily wrought into the program. During the six weeks after April 1, 1940, Anglo-French contracts aggre-

gated about four hundred million dollars, bringing
the total Allied commitments to a round billion;
and in all this the Administration—with American
sentiment strongly supporting it—cordially cooperated.

Ever since the rise of the Nazi dictatorship, the
successive aggressions of the Germans, Italians,
and Japanese had been so astutely coordinated as
to point to an alert interplay in the seizure of
opportunities if not to some rough concert of plan.
It was not to be expected that Japan would lose
the advantage which the European war gave her.
She had not done so in 1914; she would not miss
her chance in 1939–40. The Russo-German compact gave Tokyo a temporary shock, for it seemed
to free the hands of the Soviet Union for possible
hostilities in the Far East. The Japanese Government at once protested to Berlin that the new
treaty was a flagrant violation of the Anti-Comintern Pact. At the same time it hurried reinforcements to the frontiers of Outer Mongolia, where
border fighting during the summer cost the Japanese nearly 20,000 casualties.

But Russo-Japanese relations suddenly took a
new turn only less dramatic than that engineered
by Ribbentrop and Molotov in Europe. On September 16, Moscow announced that the heavy
fighting which had been proceeding all spring and
summer on the Outer Mongolian borders had been

ended by a formal truce. It was plain that as the Soviet Union was ready to divert German arms against the Western democracies in Europe, it was no less ready to give Japan a clear field against them in the Pacific. Moscow was fully aware that Japanese militarists planned to eliminate British, American, Dutch, and French influences from the "East Asia Co-Prosperity Sphere," and it contemplated such a result without displeasure.

The consequences of the changed situation were soon felt in the Far East. The heavy Japanese forces on the Outer Mongolian border, estimated as high as 600,000, began to stream back into China to help prosecute the unfinished war still raging there. While this took place, the press and radio campaign for the "new order" in the Orient was strongly pressed. The original "East Asia Co-Prosperity Sphere," generally held to denote Japan, Manchukuo, and Northern China, was being replaced by a more resounding phrase with the word "Greater" prefixed, this apparently pointing also to Indo-China, Siam, the Dutch Indies, and South China. Many civilian leaders in Japan were still willing to extend the nation's economic and political sway by gradual steps, but most military chieftains took the view that Japan must move at once—while conditions favored it—to achieve complete self-sufficiency, and to armor its new empire against attack. The British Ambassador, Craigie, tells us that by January, 1940, most Japanese leaders had reached the conclusion that they might soon have to fight the combined forces of Britain and America. To gain control of all the resources of Eastern Asia even at the risk of precipitating a conflict seemed the part of wisdom. As the Japanese watched the German war machine roll forward, their confidence in a drastic readjustment of prestige, power, and riches throughout the globe increased.

Early in 1940, therefore, Japan threw troops ashore on Hainan Island, which lay in a strategic position off the coast of French Indo-China and straddled the British lines of communication between Singapore and Hong Kong. It furnished a strong aviation base, moreover, for air raids against the vital Burma Road supply line of the Chinese Kuomintang Government. The island had previously been recognized as part of the French sphere of influence. Its occupation alarmed all the democratic powers, which at once called upon Japan for explanations and an announcement of intentions. Even while Japan was protesting that she had no intention of occupying the island permanently, she was preparing another move. On March 31, Tokyo announced the annexation of the Spratly Islands, long claimed by France and of considerable potential value as naval and aviation bases. They lay southwest of the Philippines and might well be of use in an investment of the American position in that archipelago. Plainly, expansion on the mainland was unchecked, and was carrying the sun flag southward in the direction long urged by the more aggressive naval leaders. As Japanese confidence increased, the economic warfare waged in China against Western powers, and particularly Great Britain, was intensified. Having occupied the Yangtze Valley as high as Hankow, Tokyo took steps to stifle all commerce under foreign flags and acquire a monopoly of the trade of this great waterway.

More than once the American people had been compelled to think of the possibility of war in the Atlantic, or war in the Pacific. The republic possessed a navy quite able to cope with any single power in the East or any single power in the West. But the nation now had to think of the possibility of a combined assault from two sides; for the first time in its history, it had to face the fact that, with Germany and Japan on the march, its Atlantic and Pacific coasts might be simultaneously attacked. From its long dream of complete security the country awoke with a start. As it comprehended the grim realities of the situation, peril suddenly took a long stride nearer. On May 10, 1940, news came that German troops were pouring into Holland,

Luxembourg, and Belgium, and that the first lines of defense were being breached. Hitler had proclaimed: "The fight which begins today will decide the destiny of the German people for a thousand years."

CHAPTER VIII

BETWEEN the outbreak of war in Europe and Pearl
Harbor intervened twenty-seven months of anxious American watching. That period, the more
critical because it covered a Presidential election,
fell into two clearly defined parts. During the first
eight months Americans yet hugged the belief that
the storm might quickly blow itself out. Then,
after the German sweep in the spring of 1940, they
became increasingly aware that mobilization of
national resources and direct aid to the Allies were
essential.

President Roosevelt was for three reasons anxious to see the war stopped on any tolerable terms.
First, its continuance would increase the danger
of American involvement; second, an Allied victory would probably be won only after such a
desperate contest that Europe would fall into economic collapse; and third, a victory by Hitler
would place the United States in grave danger.
Early in 1940 he sent Under Secretary Sumner

Welles to Berlin, Rome, Paris, and London to explore the possibility of peace. The mission was foredoomed to failure. For one reason, as Welles puts it, American opinion had "reached another climax of out-and-out isolationism," and it demanded that the Government "refrain from any action, and even from any gesture, which might conceivably involve the United States with the warring powers." Welles visited Berlin conscious that America's immense industrial might and military potential carried no weight, for only one factor could then have deflected Hitler, the certainty that our power "would be directed against him if he attempted to carry out his intention of conquering the world by force"; and no American representative could intimate that it would. The Under Secretary found the Nazis intent upon a crushing military victory. He found Mussolini under their spell. As he packed for home, a train carried the Duce to a new meeting with Hitler at the Brenner Pass.

The cautiousness of American sentiment was illustrated when, after the Soviet Government demanded that Finland cede its important border areas, Russian forces in November, 1939, invaded Finland. American indignation rose high. Roosevelt issued a statement placing the whole onus of the war on Moscow, and asked airplane-makers to refuse sales to Russia, which was guilty of "unprovoked bombing." Since the Neutrality Act was not applied, Congress might have granted an open loan to Finland. But while it was timidly moving toward indirect aid through the Export-Import Bank, Finland was overwhelmed, and had to sign the harsh Soviet terms on March 3, 1940.

A month later complacent sentiment on neutrality suffered its first heavy shock in the Nazi invasion of Denmark and Norway (April 8). The illusion of a "phony war" was shattered as men saw what might happen to unprepared neutrals trusting to their innocence. Secretary Morgenthau at once took over Danish and Norwegian funds to prevent their falling into Nazi hands. The position of Greenland and Iceland gave the Government great anxiety, for they might be used as stepping stones in an invasion of North America. To be sure, the British navy could swiftly seize possession, but this was not wholly desirable. The State Department took the attitude that protection could properly be extended under the Monroe Doctrine, and Secretary Morgenthau had Coast Guard forces prepare for immediate movement to the area.

The final blow to American indifference, however, was struck in May. From numerous sources in late April hints reached the State and Treasury Departments of an impending invasion of the low countries and France. A German scheme had been drafted for organizing Europe into a *Grossraum-wirtschaft*, or a planned economy on a continental scale. This involved the concentration of European industry within a Greater Germany, the virtual enslavement of the Poles, Czechs, French, and other peoples, who were to be used for food production and industrial labor but to be deprived of opportunities for higher culture, and the depopulation of wide areas for German colonization. After the New Europe had been fully organized, the Nazis would swiftly turn to other continents. They planned an offensive in the West to end the conflict by quick, heavy blows, and by the end of April rumors of the coming onslaught filled all capitals. On May 9, while the President was at dinner, Ambassador John Cudahy in Brussels telephoned him that the German invasion was under way; and the press next morning informed a startled nation that Nazi columns were pouring into Belgium and Holland.

Seldom in American history have public opinion and the national outlook changed more swiftly than in May, 1940. For parallels we have to go back to 1917 and 1861. On May 15 the Dutch capitulated; on May 28 the Belgian king surrendered; by May 30 the French armies were lost or in flight, and the British were escaping from Dunkirk. A power that had sworn hostility to democracy stood triumphant in Continental Europe. The question uppermost in American minds was whether, with overwhelming German forces on the Channel, Britain and her fleet could be saved. If they were lost, if the Germans organized the European navies, if Axis air power were concentrated at Dakar to menace South America, and if Japan poised herself for a blow in the Pacific, the United States would stand in a desperate position.

It was a time for decisive action, and the Roosevelt Administration hastened to write one of its most creditable chapters. Dutch, Belgian, and French assets in the United States were frozen. On May 16 the President went before Congress with a special defense message. Both branches crowded into the House chamber; the Cabinet took seats in the front of the hall; and in a solemn atmosphere, broken by wild bursts of cheering, he asked for immediate appropriations of nearly $900,000,-000, with authorization for contract obligations totaling nearly $300,000,000 more. The radio carried to the nation his reminder that air power had ended the era in which the Atlantic and Pacific placed a moat about the country. New England could be bombed from Greenland, and New York from Bermuda; air bases in West Africa could place Brazil under threat of subjugation; and if the Japanese overran Alaska, they would be within four hours' flying time of Seattle and Portland. "I should like," said the President, "to see this nation geared up to the ability to turn out at least 50,000 planes a year." The appropriations were immediately passed. Roosevelt appointed an advisory commission of business leaders and others to help supervise defense measures. On June 7 he issued an order sweeping away the restrictions which Secretary Harry Woodring of the War Department had placed on the sale of obsolete military equipment to Britain; and rifles, machine guns, and other arms were hurried with all speed to British ports.

As France under Paul Reynaud staggered toward the ignominious surrender of June 22, the United States pressed insistently for measures to keep the French fleet out of Nazi hands. The policy met with general success: some vessels joined the British, more were interned at Alexandria, and still others were sent to African bases. A successful British defense of Egypt and Suez was made possible and Axis control of the Atlantic prevented. When the Pétain Government was set up at Vichy in unoccupied France, the course of American policy toward France that had been set in June, 1940, was never changed. Ultimately it smoothed the way for the Anglo-American invasion of North Africa.

Meanwhile, the President had declared in a

dramatic speech at Charlottesville, Virginia, that
the United States would give the fullest possible
aid in material to the defenders of democracy; and
as a great surge of anxiety for Great Britain swept
the country, larger shipments of arms were made
available to her. Anglo-French purchasing had
been heavily expanded in April and May, and on
the fall of France the British took over the French
commitments. Emergency measures were taken to
break the machine-tool bottleneck, which in turn
made possible the breaking of the engine bottleneck in the airplane industry. On the suggestion of
the British, the defense legislation included power
to control the export and reexport of vital war
materials. When President Roosevelt on July 18
broadcast his speech of acceptance to the Democratic national convention in Chicago, he arraigned
the appeasers and he made it plain that he meant
to press on with his policy of assistance to Britain
and China. Public opinion was with him; and in
mid-August he announced—with a boldness all the
more creditable in a campaign year—that he was
negotiating with Great Britain for the lease of
naval and air bases in the Western Hemisphere.

Winston Churchill's masterly organization of
British defense thrilled the world, while his won-
derfully eloquent speeches moved American feeling
like a trumpet call. People read that desperate

British workers were toiling seventy-five and eighty hours a week in the munitions factories. Many isolationist voices were still heard; but the Republican convention, meeting in Philadelphia on June 24, turned its back squarely on Taft, Dewey, and others who leaned toward a cautious policy and nominated the forthright Wendell Willkie. A thoroughgoing internationalist, Willkie was as vigorous as Roosevelt in demanding all possible aid to Britain short of war, and resolutely insisted upon national unity in foreign affairs throughout the campaign.

One measure of preparedness and assistance swiftly followed another. Just after Dunkirk, Roosevelt had asked Congress for another billion for armaments; in early summer a third defense message called for five billions more. On June 20, the Cabinet was reorganized by the installation of two distinguished Republicans, Henry L. Stimson and Frank Knox, as Secretary of War and of the Navy respectively. At the same time the Government warned Germany and Italy to keep their hands off the French, Dutch, and Danish possessions in the New World. Von Ribbentrop rejected this warning, declaring that American intervention in Europe justified German intervention in American affairs; but a new Pan-American conference, held in Havana the last week of July, provided for

joint action in protecting and governing any territory in the Western Hemisphere over which a
European power lost control. The American republics, in short, united in declaring that no European
possession in the New World should be subject to
forced transfer to another non-American power.
Nor was this all. At Havana the delegates took
another step which went far toward making the
Monroe Doctrine a multinational doctrine. They
declared that "any attempt on the part of a non-
American state against the integrity or inviolability
of the territory, the integrity or political independence of an American state," should be regarded
as an act of aggression against *all* the New World
nations.

The United States was now allied with the Latin-
American republics against Axis aggression; and
a virtual alliance with Canada immediately followed. The President and Prime Minister Mackenzie King, meeting at Ogdensburg, New York,
on August 18, announced that the two countries
would set up a Permanent Joint Board of Defense,
to "consider in the broad sense the defense of the
north half of the Western Hemisphere." This was
followed in due course (April 20, 1941) by an
agreement for coordinating the production programs of the two countries. Congress showed its
appreciation of the public mood by passing in the
summer of 1940, at Roosevelt's request, the first

peacetime conscription law in the nation's history; a law written and voted on a bipartisan basis. This Burke-Wadsworth Act, effective September 16, made about 16,500,000 men liable to the draft for military training.

The most notable step taken by Roosevelt in the summer of 1940, however, was his arrangement with Great Britain for the exchange of destroyers against bases. Hard pressed by German submarines, the British obtained fifty over-age destroyers, and in return gave the United States ninety-nine-year leases on bases in Newfoundland, Bermuda, various West Indian islands, Trinidad, and British Guiana. Attorney-General Jackson certified that the President had Constitutional power to effect the arrangement, which (unlike Jefferson's purchase of Louisiana) was never submitted to Congress, but which met enthusiastic popular approval. This, as Roosevelt put it, was "an epochal and far-reaching act of preparation for continental defense in the face of grave danger." How grim the peril was men saw when later that month (September 27), Germany, Italy, and Japan signed a sweeping treaty of alliance. One feature of it was a provision that these powers would assist each other with their fullest resources if any one of them were attacked by a nation not then involved in the European or Far Eastern conflict; that is, by the United States. The President would have been highly censurable had he failed to take the boldest measures to ensure the national safety.*

Until early fall of 1940 it had been questionable whether Great Britain could survive, and until late fall uncertain whether Roosevelt would receive his third term. Within six weeks both issues were determined. German invasion of England was impossible without command of the air; but when a gigantic air armada was launched at the island, the gallant Royal Air Force completely smashed it. By the beginning of October the Battle of Britain had been won. This was followed by Roosevelt's decisive reelection. At once a new phase of foreign policy opened. The United States had been neutral until the fall of France; unneutral but hesitant during the dubious summer of 1940, with Roosevelt doing what he could to aid Britain but Congress still

* Reynaud had first asked for the sale or loan of destroyers just before the fall of France, while Churchill had almost simultaneously suggested the same action. The British Government began urging the subject early in the summer of 1940. Churchill wished to make an outright gift of the leases to the bases. He did not like bargaining when the life of nations hung in the balance; he preferred a generous gesture on each side. Roosevelt, however, agreed with Hull that he had no Constitutional or legal right to make gifts of public property. It was finally arranged that Great Britain would make the lease of bases in Newfoundland and Bermuda a gift, but that the Caribbean bases would be treated as an exchange for the cession of the destroyers. Roosevelt called this stroke the most important action taken in reinforcement of the national defense since the acquisition of Louisiana—which had likewise been effected without previous Congressional sanction.

largely isolationist in temper. Now the country turned to definite participation in the war, though without formal declaration of hostilities. On December 29 the President defined the new attitude in his much-applauded "arsenal of democracy" address. He told the country that it was of vital concern to America that the Axis powers should not break down Britain and overrun the Atlantic; that if they gained the mastery in Europe and the Orient, the Americas would thereafter be living at the point of a gun; that the United States must integrate its own defense with that of Great Britain and the other free nations resisting aggression; and that it must have more ships, guns, and planes to make it the great "arsenal of democracy."

It was henceforth a cardinal principle of American foreign policy that Great Britain must not be allowed to meet defeat through slow attrition. The British Government for its part engaged that if the United States would help supply the materials, it and the Dominions would use them to achieve victory. If America did not save its remaining friends, it would be left to face the triumphant aggressors on two fronts. The tripartite military alliance of Germany, Italy, and Japan had made it perfectly clear that the three aggressors regarded the United States as a common enemy, and merely bided their time for an attack. Informed men suspected what is now known, that the pact contained a secret protocol by which Japan pledged herself under certain circumstances to attack the English-speaking powers. While the Berlin foreign office called it an answer to the destroyer deal, the Tokyo *Asahi* declared that "a clash between Japan and America now seems inevitable." But even without this challenge, American opinion would have moved forward. Willkie in his last preelection speech said that everyone, Republicans, Democrats, and independents, "believe in giving aid to the heroic British people. We must make available to them the products of our industry." A Gallup poll in September had revealed that 52 per cent of the people wished to aid Britain even at the risk of war.

But what could the United States do? Britain was nearing the end of her financial resources. In the sixteen months following the outbreak of the war, she paid out nearly four and a half billion dollars to America and other lands for supplies. Her dollar assets were running so low that by mid-December of 1940 the letting of new British contracts practically stopped. Direct loans were forbidden by the Johnson Act of 1934 and the Neutrality Act of 1939, repeal of which would be difficult; moreover, experience had shown that war loans had undesirable post-war repercussions. Defeated in the air, the Germans turned to night bombing. As damage to shipping and industrial plants mounted, British needs grew more urgent. Lord Lothian, returning to the Washington Embassy from a brief trip home, announced that ships, munitions, bombers, and money were all desperately required if victory was to be won. But how supply them?

On this problem a variety of Administration leaders—the President, Hull, Morgenthau, Harry Hopkins, and others—exercised their wits; so did various men in London. As early as August 20, Churchill hinted at a broad scheme of American help, while in September the London *Times* referred to "a larger strategic plan for mutual assistance in self-defense which is now being worked out." Treasury lawyers found an old statute of 1892 which permitted the Secretary of War to lease army property, when not required for public use, for five years or less. The President independently hit upon the idea of lending material. Mentioning it at an early date to Secretary Morgenthau, he developed it in a post-election discussion with Harry Hopkins. A fire was raging, he told Hopkins; the British and their Allies were fighting it. What does a householder do when his neighbor's place is in flames? He lends hose, ladders, and axes to fight their spread. On December 17, the very day that Morgenthau told a House subcommittee that the British were at the end of their financial tether, the President expounded his idea to a press conference, and he developed it at another as the month ended. The Government, he proposed, should drop the dollar sign, take control over production for war, and lend or sell under mortgage whatever planes, ships, guns, and other materials Great Britain needed, with some form of replacement to take place later. But all thought of repayment in kind was soon replaced by the idea of mutual aid.

This conception was a brilliant inspiration, and the country rallied to it. The President's annual message of January 6, 1941, outlined the plan in detail; and while Harry Hopkins went to England to confer with Churchill on implementing it, a bill was pressed through Congress. In vain did such isolationists as Burton K. Wheeler, Hamilton Fish, and Charles A. Beard oppose it. On March 11 the Lend-Lease Act (significantly entitled H.R. 1776), passed Congress by a wide margin, 260 to 165 in the House, 60 to 31 in the Senate; and with it soon passed a seven-billion-dollar appropriation bill. The law authorized the President to designate as a beneficiary any country whose defense he deemed vital to the defense of the United States. For this country he might manufacture or procure any material of war, and then sell, exchange, lease, lend, or even give such materials. The country named might refit its ships in American ports, and might receive defense information from the United States.

Seldom if ever has a broader enactment been placed upon the statute books.

With this Act the period of neutrality ended, and a brief phase of quasi-belligerency opened. The country was now awake. The phrase "all aid short of war" had dropped from general use, for most citizens were ready to give Britain and China full aid even if it meant war. "Today, at last," said Roosevelt, in an address to the nation four days after the passage, "ours is not a partial effort. It is a total effort. . . . Our country is going to play its full part." As the bill moved through Congress, the country had been encouraged by the doughty resistance of the Greeks against the Italians and by dazzling British victories in Libya. The situation soon changed for the worse: April found the British forced back to the borders of Egypt, and the Germans overrunning Yugoslavia and Greece. But with the ample funds voted by Congress, the shipping of lend-lease aid shortly reached large volume.

The next logical step was the protection of the shipments. It was obviously useless to manufacture guns and airplanes for Britain only to let them be sunk in mid-Atlantic. On March 15 the President announced in a radio speech that the Government would maintain a bridge of ships to Britain and Greece. The next day Senator Carter Glass declared in favor of armed convoys if the Administration wanted them, and the day after that the Committee to Defend America by Aiding the Allies came out for convoys. As yet Roosevelt was unwilling to take so radical a step. On April 9, however, the United States signed an agreement with the Danish Minister for the occupation of Greenland, as part of the sphere of cooperative Hemispheric defense, and for the establishment there of naval and air bases. A fortnight later, Roosevelt announced that neutrality patrols would be sent as far out into the Atlantic as might be necessary for the defense of the Western Hemisphere. On May 27, proclaiming a state of unlimited national emergency, he announced that America would "actively resist" every attempt by the Nazis to gain control of the seas, that the patrol was being extended indefinitely, and that it was being strengthened by more ships and planes. It was manifest that a clear difference existed between convoys and patrols; but it was also manifest that when patrols became sufficiently broad and numerous, they furnished as much protection as convoys.

At this uneasy point, the trend of the war was sharply changed by a supreme act of German folly. Ever since their armies partitioned Poland, Germany and Russia had glared at each other suspiciously. They had a non-aggression pact, they exchanged vows of amity, and Russian shipments helped sustain the German armies; but they had no faith in continued friendship. Russian expansion

worried Hitler—the Soviet Union had taken over
not only eastern Poland, but the Baltic states, Bes-
sarabia, and Bukovina; Hitler believed that Russia
had encouraged Yugoslavia in resistance to Germany. Molotov made one last-minute effort to
preserve the peace. According to documents later
captured by American forces in Germany (Frank-
furt dispatch, New York *Times*, March 19, 1946),
he visited Berlin a few weeks before the Nazis were
ready to attack. Here he offered Germany a full
military alliance in return for permanent annexation of the territories already occupied by Russia,
complete control of the Dardanelles, a free hand in
Iran and Iraq, and a sufficient area of Saudi Arabia
to give the Soviet Union control of the Persian
Gulf. Hitler regarded these demands as excessive.
He knew that Russia would remain undependable.
Britain and America had warned Moscow that a
blow was impending, and it came June 22, 1941.
Confident of their ability to conquer Russia in a
few months, the Nazi legions crossed the border
in an attack that at first carried down all resistance.

Without hesitation, both the American and British Governments moved to assist Russia. While
they had no illusions as to the character of the dictatorship in Moscow, they had faith in the Russian
people. The hard-pressed British at once spared
some of their war materials for the Russian forces.
The United States without delay extended lend-

lease to the Soviet Union. Just how important this help was it is impossible to say; but it seems certain that it contributed heavily to the mounting resistance of Russia.

As the summer of 1941 witnessed the rapid development of Hitler's drive to the very gates of Moscow and Leningrad, it found the situation in the North Atlantic moving to a point where war seemed imminent and unescapable. In May an American merchantman, the *Robin Moor,* was sunk by a German submarine. In August another American-owned vessel, the *Sessa,* was sent to the bottom by torpedo and shells, while on September 4 the destroyer *Greer* was attacked. Roosevelt on September 11 declared that the navy would henceforth "shoot the rattlesnakes of the Atlantic" without waiting for them to attack, and that American patrols would maintain the freedom of the seas in "waters we deem necessary for our defense"—a phrase not precisely defined. Men now widely accepted the doctrine that the United States, having produced enormous supplies of lend-lease for Britain, must see them safely delivered. "The American navy," said Secretary Knox on September 15, "will provide protection as adequate as we can make it for ships of every flag carrying lend-lease supplies between the American continent and the waters adjacent to Iceland"; and these waters were all but adjacent to the British Isles. American forces had been landed in Iceland early in July to supplement, and later to replace, the British forces which had garrisoned that island against Nazi attack. American patrols were sweeping at least halfway across the Atlantic.

The country waited for an incident on the high seas which would carry it into full belligerency. On October 17 the Navy Department announced that the destroyer *Kearny* had been hit by a torpedo; eleven sailors had been killed, it turned out, and ten injured. The President declared that "the shooting had started." He had asked Congress to give him the right to arm merchant vessels and to lift the ban on the entrance of American ships into the war zone. Against this step the isolationists made another bitter fight. Early in November the desired legislation passed the Senate 50 to 37, and the House 212 to 194; figures which show how reluctant Congress was to court a conflict. But fortunately for national unity, flagrant war did not yet begin. It was on the other side of the globe that the decisive blow was to fall.

When the Nazis invaded Poland, Japan was still pressing her campaign for the subjugation of China and still treating foreign interests in that country with arrogant hostility. Growing tired of endless protests, Washington in July, 1939, had decided upon more drastic steps, and had given Japan the required six months' notice of the termination of the old commercial treaty of 1911. The United States was thus free to place an embargo on shipments of materials to Japan and to adopt other retaliatory steps. This sudden blow, shocking the Tokyo Ministry, was received in different ways in different quarters. The Japanese public as a whole thought the action unfair and irritating; traders and industrialists took it as a notice that a changed policy leading to a new commercial treaty was needed; while the militarists saw in it proof of the wisdom of their plan for making Japan self-sufficient by establishing political and economic hegemony over the Orient. By the time the commercial treaty expired in January, 1940, the Japanese rulers, according to Sir Robert Craigie, decided "that they must be prepared to fight the United States and the British Empire jointly."

With the fall of France, Japanese policy naturally stiffened. Nearly all groups in Tokyo held that the Rome–Berlin Axis was assured of victory; that the French, British, and Dutch empires were collapsing. Prince Konoye, returning to power in July, 1940, set up a government more completely dominated by militarist influences than any in the previous decade. Frantic energy was displayed in rearmament. But no longer were most of the huge sums for the army and navy employed in the Chinese adventure; roughly three-quarters of them went into preparations for a more ambitious scheme of conquest. As Foreign Minister, Konoye selected Yosuke Matsuoka, who had been educated as a boy and youth in America, had spent long years in the Japanese foreign service, representing his country at the Paris Peace Conference and leading its delegation out of the League hall after the Assembly's vote of censure on Manchuria, and had become head of the South Manchuria Railroad. The small, swarthy, bullet-headed man, garrulous, shrewd, and full of vindictive prejudices, had two stubborn delusions: one that Britain was already defeated, and the other that the United States could be bluffed into a course of timid neutrality in Europe and Asia. In Hull's phrase, Matsuoka was as crooked as a basket of fishhooks.

Intimidation was precisely the policy least likely to succeed with the United States. As early as September 12, 1940, Ambassador Grew telegraphed the State Department that "further conciliatory measures would be futile and unwise," for Tokyo was impressed as it saw "the United States and Great Britain steadily growing together in measures of mutual defense." Japan, he thought, might be dissuaded from war by a "strong" American stand. In December he wrote the President that unless America was prepared to get out of the Orient bag and baggage, it was "bound eventually to come to a head-on clash with the Japanese." The tripartite pact of Germany, Italy, and Japan in

September, 1940, was plainly aimed at America, and the United States was aware from the beginning of 1941 that Japanese militarists were preparing for hostilities. In January, President Roosevelt sent Grew a significant letter. Replying to the Ambassador's suggestion that an American–Japanese war might fatally reduce aid to Britain, he declared that on the other hand, if Britain lost such a vital base as Singapore, the resultant weakening of her whole imperial position might bring about her defeat in Europe.

Certain sequels of the tripartite pact were ominous. Japan was drawn more and more tightly into the Axis grip. Germany obviously expected that, if the United States made a sudden "attack" on the Axis, Japan would (as the pact provided) come to Hitler's assistance. Still more, Berlin hoped that Japanese menaces would prevent the United States from entering the war until it was too late—until Britain was vanquished. Japanese military and naval missions at once hurried to Berlin and Rome to pick up the latest information on strategy and equipment. German experts in aircraft-building, naval warfare, and military devices were sent by hundreds to Japan. Gestapo men and Nazi secret service agents assisted Konoye in erecting an efficient police and espionage organization. Matsuoka himself, traveling to Berlin, meanwhile poured out his hopes and plans to Hitler on April 4, 1941.

The chief fear of the State Department at this moment was that Japan would drive southward to overwhelm French Indo-China, British Malaysia, Singapore, and the Dutch East Indies. Economic motives for such action were now strong. By the beginning of 1941 the American embargoes were exerting a painful pressure on Japan. Shipments of iron, steel, most other important metals, and high octane gasoline had been stopped; and petroleum exports were still permitted only to deprive Tokyo of an excuse for seizing East Asian oil supplies. Early in the year Japan grasped an opportunity to mediate a boundary dispute between Thailand (Siam) and French Indo-China, and soon afterward took virtual control of Thailand affairs. A new Ambassador, Admiral Kichisaburo Nomura, was sent to Washington. A cultivated and honest man, he wished for peace. Relations between him and Hull were personally cordial. But American defense officers had succeeded in deciphering the Japanese code. Messages from Tokyo to the Axis and to Nomura were constantly intercepted and laid before the State Department; and they proved that Tokyo, while talking of peace in Washington, was proceeding with plans for an aggressive expansion in Asia.

The great opportunity of the Japanese militarists opened before them when on June 22, 1941, Hitler invaded Russia. The Siberian flank of Japan was thus rendered secure. Matsuoka had paused in Moscow (April, 1941) to sign a Soviet–Japanese treaty by which each nation agreed to remain neutral if the other became involved in war with a third power; but treaties could be broken, and Tokyo now expected to see Russia crushed. Ten days after the invasion, the Japanese Emperor presided over a conference which adopted a "crucial national policy." Its character was revealed when early in July orders were issued for complete mobilization to wage total war, and preparations were made to strike southward. Late that month the abject Vichy Government in France granted Japan the right to establish air and naval bases in southern Indo-China and garrison troops there. Acting Secretary Welles protested that this was done under Japanese pressure, and that it lent assistance to Germany in her policy of world conquest; the British Ambassador and Australian Minister in Tokyo offered unequivocal warnings of the dangers that Japan was incurring—but all to no avail. At the end of July, Japanese troops began to pour into southern Indo-China. By occupying Camranh Bay the Japanese Navy obtained an excellent base only 750 miles from Singapore, while its airfields at Cambodia Point were but 500 miles from the great British port. The Japanese shadow was falling on all southeastern Asia—even on India.

The tense final act in the drama had now

opened. It was vital to the security of the Americans in the Philippines, the Dutch in the East Indies, and the British in Malaysia and Burma that the Japanese be persuaded to halt and withdraw. Up to this point the American Government had permitted oil exports to Japan, reasoning that their interruption would give Tokyo grounds for moving against the oil fields of the Netherlands Indies. Now, against the advice of Admiral Stark and other naval experts who feared that such action would increase the war party in Japan, the President resolved to apply economic sanctions. On July 26, after publicly stating that the period of appeasement was over, he issued an executive order freezing Japanese assets in the United States. All financial transactions and import-export activities involving Japan were thus placed under Government control; cargoes and passengers were immobilized; and trade and intercourse with Japan abruptly halted. Britain and her Dominions took the same step. Japan retaliated by freezing British and American assets throughout the wide territories she now controlled. By mid-August the mobilization of the Japanese army and navy had been completed, and the fleet had begun to assemble for war games in which, as was disclosed later, the attack on Pearl Harbor was rehearsed. All Americans and Britons in Japanese-dominated areas were placed under sharp restrictions.

The Japanese war machine, fast gathering power and momentum, stood poised for some great movement. Would it strike at Siam, at the Dutch Indies, at British Malaysia, at the Americans in the Philippines and Hawaii? No one knew—the only certainty was that, unless some last-minute intervention proved effective, it would strike somewhere.

From Konoye's memoirs, written after the conflict, we have learned that the War Minister did his utmost to precipitate action, insisting that unless the American Government consented to Japan's expansionist plans, war must be provoked. Konoye also tells us that another Imperial conference was held on September 6, at which it was agreed that, unless by October 1 diplomatic action seemed to be gaining Japan's objects, "decision shall be made to go to war with the United States." All this deeply grieved Konoye.

The one hope for peace lay in diplomatic conversations between Hull and the Japanese Ambassador, Nomura, which had begun in the spring of 1941. President Roosevelt took an important part in the exchanges, proposing on July 24 the neutralization of Indo-China. This proposal the Japanese Government, anxious to exploit its occupation to the full in the military, political, and economic spheres, refused to accept. In August, Roosevelt and Churchill agreed that Britain and the United States should issue parallel warnings to Tokyo.

Nothing could have been more emphatic than the document which the President handed Ambassador Nomura on August 17. After pointing out that Japan had continued its military activities in China and Indo-China, this paper declared "that if the Japanese Government takes any further steps in pursuance of a policy or program of military domination by force or threat of force of neighboring countries, the Government of the United States will be compelled to take immediately any and all steps which it may deem necessary toward safeguarding the legitimate rights and interests of the United States and American nationals, and toward insuring the safety and security of the United States." Prince Konoye, frightened by the rapid drift toward war, was beyond question eager to draw back. With Cabinet support, he proposed (August 27) a meeting between himself and Roosevelt at sea in a supreme effort to reach a settlement. But while Roosevelt was willing to travel thousands of miles to see Konoye, he and Hull felt that a preliminary agreement on principles was necessary; and the defiant attitude of the Japanese militarists made this impossible.

On three basic points, in fact, every American effort in September and October to reach an understanding was frustrated. One was the question of Japan's reversion to a fundamentally peaceful course, which involved withdrawal from Indo-China. One was the question of Japanese commitments to Germany under the tripartite pact, for Tokyo continued by implication to threaten that if the United States went to war on behalf of Britain, she would go to war on behalf of Hitler. The third question was of a Sino-Japanese settlement, and especially of definite pledges of evacuation of China by Japanese troops. On none of these issues would the militarists consent to pledges of the kind Washington demanded. According to Konoye's memoirs, the War Minister at a council on October 12 flatly refused to consider troop evacuation from the mainland.

The resignation of the despairing Konoye on October 18 was evidence that the sands were running out. General Hideiki Tojo, twice War Minister, a professional army man known for his incisive qualities as "the Razor," became Prime Minister, and chose Shigenori Togo, a career diplomatist, as Foreign Minister. In early life Tojo had served as Assistant Military Attaché in Berlin, while Togo had a German wife; both men felt certain of Nazi success and both reflected the views of the army. A momentary hope that Tojo might better matters by exercising a larger restraint over extremists than Konoye had been able to furnish soon died away. On November 3, Grew pointed out the necessity for estimating realistically "Japan's obvious preparations to implement an alternative program in the

event the peace program fails"; and he declared
that action "which might render unavoidable an
armed conflict with the United States may come
with dangerous and dramatic suddenness." On
November 7, Secretary Hull reported in detail to
the Cabinet, describing the imminent danger of
Japanese attack; and so keen was the sense of peril
that Roosevelt called upon each member for his
opinion of the situation. They agreed that high officials should make speeches to arouse the country
to its danger, and within the next few days the
President, Secretary Knox, and Under Secretary
Welles did so.

It is now known that Japanese plans for the
Pearl Harbor attack were completed by September 18, and that early in October Tokyo decided
that if peace moves did not succeed by November
25, the attack should take place on December 7,
American time. In mid-November an able career
diplomat, Saburo Kurusu, arrived in Washington
from Tokyo to assist Ambassador Nomura. He was
an unfortunate choice. Ambassador at Berlin in the
fall of 1940, he had been one of the signers of the
tripartite pact; a rigid nationalist, a cunning
plotter, and a believer in Nazi victory, he was
totally incapable of understanding the American
point of view. Hull at once decided that he was
deceitful. In his talks with the Secretary and the
President he proved stiff, cold, and unhelpful. After

repeated conferences, on November 20 he and Nomura presented what Hull knew, from intercepted
Tokyo messages, was Japan's final offer—her ulti-
matum.

This document was entirely unacceptable. In
return for a promise to withdraw Japanese troops
from southern to northern Indo-China, and to refrain from further advances in southeast Asia or
the southwest Pacific, Tokyo demanded that the
United States cease to give China material and
moral aid; restore commercial relations with Japan;
supply the Japanese with "a required quantity of
oil"; and press the Netherlands Indies to furnish
Japan with oil and other supplies. Kurusu flatly
refused to abrogate the tripartite pact, or to give
up, in effect, a victor's peace in China; the United
States was to refrain from doing anything to prejudice a restoration of peace between China and
Japan. Hull regarded these demands as involving
an American surrender. He at once set to work to
draft broad proposals for a temporary agreement
or *modus vivendi*, to last three months while a
permanent agreement was being negotiated.

This *modus vivendi*, drafted November 21 and
22, would have constituted a decidedly generous
offer on the part of the United States; indeed, the
Chinese Government thought it all too generous.
In essence, it provided that both Japan and the
United States should direct their policies toward

lasting peace; that both should refrain from making further advances in the Pacific area; and that an approach toward the resumption of normal trade should begin at once. Japan was to withdraw from southern Indo-China and reduce her forces in northern Indo-China to 25,000. The United States was to open its doors to imports from Japan, to export to Japan $600,000 worth of raw cotton monthly, to ship petroleum for civilian use, and to send in food and medical supplies. But the document had a purely academic interest. The Chinese Government reacted vigorously against it. Chiang Kai-shek protested earnestly to Washington and London. At the same time, Hull realized that a great part of American public opinion would oppose supplying even limited quantities of oil to Japan. He therefore gave up the *modus vivendi.* Instead, he resolved to revert to fundamentals. He would present to Japan a ten-point draft of a basic agreement for a lasting peace. President Roosevelt read his memorandum and approved it. After all, why bother with a three months' arrangement? Why not fix the essentials for an enduring friendship?—if Japan could be brought to accept them.

The American counter-offer, which went to the Japanese envoys on November 26, was a plan for a broad, honest, peaceful settlement. The United States suggested that Japan should withdraw her forces from southern Indo-China, and reduce those in northern Indo-China to 25,000; that both countries should promise not to advance further in the Pacific area; and that they should exchange mutual pledges directed toward a lasting peace. An outline of more permanent terms included a multilateral non-aggression pact among the Pacific powers; an agreement to respect the territorial integrity of Indo-China and the open door there; agreement to support no regime in China but that of the National Government (Chiang Kai-shek); withdrawal of Japanese forces from China and Indo-China; relinquishment of extra-territorial rights in China; an agreement not to interpret a pact with any other country (e.g., the tripartite pact) in a way which clashed with the basic accord; a liberal Japanese-American trade agreement; removal of freezing measures and stabilization of the dollar-yen rate. In short, this agreement recognized the sovereignty and territorial integrity of China, assured the freedom of other Pacific areas from aggression, and promised a complete restoration of trade relations and economic cooperation. From additional intercepts of Japanese messages, Hull knew that the deadline had been extended to November 29, Tokyo time. "The sword of Damocles that hung over our heads," he writes, "was therefore attached to a clockwork set to the hour." At a later date the Secretary presented a mass of evidence to show that the Japanese communication of November 20 had really been Tokyo's last word, and that even had he made greater concessions on the 26th, they would have availed nothing. Any greater concessions would have meant that the United States consented to a second Munich.

"I am not very hopeful," Roosevelt cabled Churchill on November 24, "and we must all be prepared for real trouble, possibly soon." When Kurusu read the State Department's proposals, he declared that he believed this meant the end; that Tokyo would reject them out of hand. He was right. On the 27th the American intelligence intercepted a message from Foreign Minister Togo to Nomura and Kurusu saying that negotiations would be ruptured, but that they were to conceal this from the State Department, pretending that they were awaiting instructions. Japan, as it was learned later, had already (November 25) started her naval forces on their fateful mission against Hawaii.

Although as December opened, Roosevelt and Hull still cherished some faint hopes for peace, they knew that a sudden Japanese attack on the British, the Dutch, or the Americans was possible. They knew, through still another intercept, that the Japanese Ambassador in Berlin had been instructed to see Hitler and tell him that there was "extreme danger that war may suddenly break out between the Anglo-Saxon nations and Japan." The general belief in Washington circles was that the first blow would fall on the British and Dutch possessions. On December 6, Roosevelt, hearing that a large Japanese naval force with thirty-five transports was moving southward from Indo-China, dispatched a personal telegram to the Japanese Emperor calling attention to the "tragic possibilities" of the situation, and asking his help in restoring the traditional amity of the two nations. That evening the decoding of the first thirteen parts of the intercepted Japanese message in reply to Hull's memorandum of the 26th convinced the President that, as he told Harry Hopkins, war was at hand; and he so telephoned Admiral Stark.

The Pacific fleet lay in Pearl Harbor, President Roosevelt having decided to base it there as a deterrent to Japan rather than keep it, as some officers wished, on the California coast. Neither the military nor naval command had made proper preparations for a surprise attack. Anchored side by side in double rank, without steam to move, long lines of warships presented a perfect target; on Hickham Field scores of American battle planes were nicely aligned for assailants to destroy. At 7:55 A.M. on Sunday, December 7, the first wave of 135 Japanese bombers swept in to rain their missiles on carefully mapped objectives. Five battleships were sunk, and three others heavily damaged; three destroyers, a minelayer, and a floating drydock went down, while other vessels were hard hit. For the time being the main line of American naval defense in the Pacific was almost wiped out. The nation had suffered the greatest naval defeat in all its history. The negligence of naval and military officers had cost it a great fleet, and the loss of several thousand lives.

Meanwhile, in Washington that same Sunday Nomura had telephoned Secretary Hull to ask for an interview at one o'clock—the very hour that the blow was to be delivered in Hawaii. The interview finally took place shortly after two o'clock when Roosevelt had just telephoned the Secretary the first unconfirmed news of the attack. The two envoys handed Hull the Japanese reply to the American offer of November 26, a rambling tissue of mendacities which he characterized with fitting vigor.

"I must say that in all my conversations with you during the last nine months I have never uttered one word of untruth. This is borne out absolutely by the record. In all my fifty years of public service I have never seen a document that was more crowded with infamous falsehoods and distortions—infamous falsehoods and distortions on a scale so huge that I never imagined until today that any government on this planet was capable of uttering them."

War had come; but if it had to come, it could not have been in a better way. The treacherous

Japanese onslaught unified the nation as no other event could have done. In 1917 a large minority had protested against America's entry into the First World War; in 1941 the whole country was eager to defeat the Axis as a prelude to a new and better era. Responsible statesmen like Churchill noted, too, how fortunate it was that by long negotiations America had delayed the Japanese attack. If Tokyo had declared war against the United States and Great Britain in June, 1940, just after the French collapse, the ordeal ahead might well have been fearful. As it was, in the eighteen months since Dunkirk the United States, the British Commonwealth, and their friends had found time to rally their forces and prepare for action.

CHAPTER IX

THE DIPLOMACY OF WARTIME COOPERATION

On the grim Monday after Pearl Harbor, President Roosevelt, haggard from a long night of conferences and worry, faced a Congress that still seemed a little dazed by events. "Yesterday, December 7, 1941, a date which will live in infamy," he began; and proceeding to describe the Japanese stroke, he called upon Congress and the country to make very sure that this form of treachery should never endanger the republic again. The next day, in a radio address to the nation, he declared that Americans had learned a terrible lesson; the lesson that their ocean-girt Hemisphere was not immune from assault, and that no country could be secure in a world ruled by the principles of gangsterism. He voiced a confident prediction: "We are going to win the war and we are going to win the peace that follows." At the same time he laid down the most basic of the many prerequisites to victory. Germany and Japan, he said, "are conducting their military and naval operations in accordance with a joint plan." The United States must similarly conduct its war in close unison with its Allies. The grand strategy of the Axis powers, he said, "can be matched only with similar grand strategy."

On both sides of the titanic conflict a grand alliance swiftly took shape. Germany and Italy at once declared war upon the United States. Congress had hardly passed its joint resolution recognizing the state of war that Tokyo had thrust upon the United States before Great Britain declared war against Japan. Canada, Australia, and New Zealand at once followed. American policy had long since made sure of Latin-American good will. Before the week ended, nine nations of Central America and the West Indies had joined in the war on the Axis, and other Latin-American countries were soon to follow.

American diplomacy, in the tense period which now opened, was the diplomacy of coordination. A working wartime alliance of the loose congeries of peoples soon to be known as the United Nations had to be hammered out. It was an immense initial advantage that the English-speaking peoples had gone so far in integrating their effort. The previous August had witnessed one of the most dramatic episodes of the time, the secret meeting of Roosevelt and Churchill in a Newfoundland bight to agree upon a statement of war aims which became historic as the Atlantic Charter. Accompanied by their naval, military, and air advisers, the two governmental chiefs had drawn up a declaration of "certain common principles" on which they based their hopes for a better world. Men's imaginations were stirred by the sudden revelation of this meeting, and the story of how the statesmen had joined the crews of two warships in Sunday service on the deck of the *Prince of Wales*, singing "Onward, Christian Soldiers." Still more was the popular imagination of free people stirred by the resounding principles set forth: the destruction of tyranny, the freedom of the seas, the guarantee of free access to raw materials, the abandonment of force, and the establishment of a world-wide system of mutual security.

By the date of Pearl Harbor, the United States, Canada, and Great Britain had already created a well-planned defensive system for the North Atlantic area. American patrols covered the broad sea lanes from New York and Boston to Greenland, Iceland, and the fringes of the Shetlands. The Canadian-American Defense Board, holding repeated meetings, had drawn up detailed plans for joint action by the Dominion and the United States. American bases were being developed, with British cooperation, in Newfoundland, Bermuda, Jamaica, the Bahamas, Antigua, St. Lucia, Trinidad, and Guiana. British warships were being repaired in American yards. Lend-lease supplies had

been used for the construction of seaplane and
destroyer bases for the British in Scotland and
Northern Ireland, the United States furnishing
money, machinery, and more than a thousand engineers and mechanics. The flow of other lend-lease
materials, munitions, food, and guns was becoming
a heavy flood. Large numbers of American experts
had been poured into London, and British experts
into Ottawa and Washington, to coordinate the
activities of the three Governments. In short, a
close Anglo–American union had taken form.

This was well, for the first year of the war after
Pearl Harbor was disastrous in the extreme. Americans realized the truth of Roosevelt's stern ad-
monition: It was a war which they might lose. Indeed, in the first three months the United States
lost Guam and Wake to Japan, the enemy seized
Hong Kong and Singapore, most of the Philippines
were overrun, the strategic points in the Dutch
East Indies were seized, and even India and Australia were menaced. Not until the Battle of Mid-
way in June, 1942, turned back a Japanese force,
were the Hawaiian Islands safe. Not until the
equally victorious Battle of the Coral Sea took
place in May could the people of Australia draw a
free breath. Meanwhile, Hitler was making his
supreme effort to destroy Russian resistance, and
for a time seemed about to succeed. Marshal Rom-
mel carried the Nazi flag across North Africa to the

outer defenses of Alexandria. The Atlantic was scoured by submarines which for a time littered the American coast with sunken ships. It was not until the very end of 1942, when the British won their decisive victory at El Alamein, when the Russians stemmed the German tide at Stalingrad, and when Anglo-American forces broke ashore in North Africa, that the skies began to brighten.

The beginning of 1942 found twenty-six nations aligned against the Axis; a list destined ere the war ended to be nearly doubled. They commanded by far the greater part of the population and materials of the world. It had seemed to Secretary Hull— who for once took an initiative that would have been more characteristic of Roosevelt—important to bind these countries together in a declaration of unity for victory and justice. His subordinates, A. A. Berle, M. M. Hamilton, and Herbert Feis, drafted the main points of what became the Joint Declaration of the United Nations. President Roosevelt and Prime Minister Churchill, among others, then went over it. The name United Nations occurred to the President one morning, and he instantly carried it to the Prime Minister, then taking a bath in the White House, who assented to it! On New Year's Day Roosevelt, Churchill, Litvinov, and T. V. Soong signed the document for the four major powers. Next day representatives of the remaining twenty-two nations appended their signatures.

Well might the Czech Minister, so overcome with emotion that he had to pause some minutes before he wrote his name, say that it was the most important document he had ever signed; for this was the germ of a mighty new world organization. Each Government pledged itself to employ its full resources against the enemy. Each promised to conclude no separate peace. Each accepted the principles of the Atlantic Charter and agreed to cooperate with the other signatories. This solemn Declaration was much more than a war measure, for it looked forward to the establishment of a stronger and better League; and though it was not ratified by the Senate, it was so fervently accepted by public sentiment that it was regarded as a binding national commitment. Even more than the Atlantic Charter, it was symbolic of what Churchill called a majestic fact, "the marshalling of the good forces of the world against the evil forces," and the beginning of the climb of the toiling masses of all continents "out of the miseries into which they have been plunged, back to the broad highroad of freedom and justice."

Lend-lease was rapidly broadened by a series of master agreements into a world-wide system of mutual aid. The first such arrangement for reciprocal lend-lease was signed by Great Britain on

February 23, 1942. The previous summer a Soviet military mission had arrived in Washington to negotiate for assistance and had been disappointed by the slow progress of much American military production. But the Administration was eager to help the Soviet Union; a mission headed by William Averell Harriman proceeded to Moscow, accompanied by a British delegation, to draw up a protocol pledging supplies; and Roosevelt offered a billion-dollar credit, without interest, to the Soviet Government. In June, 1942, Russia signed a master lend-lease agreement on the same basis as that accepted by Britain and China. During 1942, the United States and Britain combined sent Russia 3,052 planes, 4,048 tanks, and huge quantities of other equipment.

It was with Britain and the Dominions that American cooperation naturally remained closest. Hull had proposed a Supreme War Council, but Roosevelt decided that for at least a time it was better to work on a regional basis. Prime Minister Churchill, reaching Washington on December 22, 1941, brought with him Field Marshal Sir John Dill, Admiral Sir Dudley Pound, and other members of the highest British command for land, sea, and air. These able men took up strategic discussions with their counterparts in the American forces. Roosevelt and Churchill at once created the Combined Chiefs of Staff, with headquarters in Washington, to integrate the strategic activities of the two countries and oversee all field operations. The American members included General George Marshall, General H. H. Arnold, Admiral Harold I. Stark, and Admiral Ernest King. A Munitions Assignment Board was almost simultaneously established, to act on the principle that the entire munitions resources of Britain and the United States would constitute a single pool. Its two initial chairmen were Harry Hopkins and Lord Beaverbrook, and before long it set up committees in Canada, Australia, and India. The work of bringing America and the British Commonwealth into almost perfect wartime unison was completed by the erection of a Combined Raw Materials Board, a Combined Shipping Adjustment Board, a Combined Production and Resources Board, and a Combined Food Board. Without their labors, the massive Anglo-American offensives of 1942–45 would have been impossible. While membership was confined to the United States, Britain, and Canada, other nations were consulted whenever their interests were involved.

No feature of the war, indeed, was more remarkable than the high degree of harmony attained by Americans and Britons as allies. All previous history had shown that alliances bred endless quarrels and misunderstandings. But throughout the war Roosevelt and Churchill worked together with a trust and friendliness that approached affection. Unified commands were set up for the Mediterranean, European, Southwest Pacific, and Southeast Asia theatres; and though subordinate commanders sometimes clashed, though Montgomery and Patton showed prima donna jealousies, though "Vinegar Joe" Stilwell raged against British, American, and Chinese superiors impartially, concord was the general rule. Eisenhower in particular, refusing to brook the slightest quarrel, achieved a fine working concert, and won the admiration of Britons from King to costermonger. The Combined Boards agreed marvelously. "Each day, each week," wrote Herbert Feis, "the British and American representatives find it possible to reach full agreement on some specific points which determine whether their respective military forces will have more equipment or less, whether greater burdens will be laid on their respective treasuries or less, whether their respective peoples will have to make more sacrifices or less. Their decisions seem generally to have recommended themselves to their governments and to the public."

Churchill, even more popular in the United States than in Britain, paid repeated visits to Washington with lighthearted informality. Twice he addressed joint sessions of Congress; he made the White House his home; he and his aides conferred endlessly with key Americans. Long conferences between President and Prime Minister in Washington in June, 1942, laid the basis for the invasion of North Africa the following November. This invasion, as much a political and psychological campaign as a military movement, was primarily Churchill's idea, for he thought the Allies unready for a cross-channel assault, and preferred an attack on Europe from the south. Completely successful in bringing the North African coast under Anglo–American control, it marked (as he said) "the end of the beginning." When in January, 1943, Roosevelt flew to Casablanca for renewed conferences, Churchill and he settled urgent military questions together, attempted to bring the French leaders De Gaulle and Giraud into harmony, and took steps to heighten the Anglo–American influence over Turkey. Stalin remained in Moscow to direct the Russian operations. In May, 1943, the Prime Minister was once more back in Washington, and the following August found him, Roosevelt, Hull, Anthony Eden, and Mackenzie King deliberating at Quebec. Here they discussed the terms of Italian surrender, relations with the Vichy regime in France, and other questions. Here, too, Hull showed Eden the draft of a Four-Power Declaration which would bind the United States, Britain, Russia, and China together after the war in establishing a new organization for peace and collective security.

With Russia, a country which had long distrusted

the United States quite as much as most Amercans distrusted Moscow, no cordiality of relations was possible. Before Pearl Harbor the Russian pact with Hitler and the Russian aggression against Finland had inspired general American condemnation. After America entered the conflict, Russian refusal to disclose military secrets, Russian reluctance to offend Japan, and Russian press attacks on prominent Americans aroused as much irritation in the United States as the Anglo–American delay in opening a second front created in the Soviet Union. On May 22, 1943, the Soviet Government dissolved the Comintern, a step which greatly pleased the democracies; but faith in the permanence of the step was slight—and its eventual revival as the Cominform caused no surprise. The head of the American military mission to Moscow 1943–45, General John R. Deane, became convinced that the unvarying strategic aim of the Soviet leaders was world Communism, to be directed from Moscow.

The military effort of Russia was enormously impressive. After Stalingrad, the Soviet retreat was transformed into a broad advance which steadily pushed the Germans westward. With a superiority in manpower of at least three to two, the Russians found it easy to throw great masses of troops at weak German points. In the revival of Russian strength from its low ebb in 1941–42, American and British shipments of material (and the moral encouragement which they brought) were highly important. Between the beginning of October, 1941, and the end of May, 1945, the United States sent 2,660 ships to Russia, loaded with more than 16,- 500,000 tons of supplies. In this period America furnished the Soviet Union with 1,966 steam and Diesel locomotives, and more than 11,000 railway cars; it sent about 440,000 trucks and combat vehicles; it supplied more than a billion dollars' worth of machinery and industrial equipment. Britain and America sent in huge quantities of guns, ammunition, airplanes, and petroleum. Without this assistance, the mobility and striking power of the Soviet forces would have been far smaller. The magnitude of the aid was little publicized in the Russian press.

The Russian Government, consistently suspicious of the Americans and British, and constantly alert to push its own political fortunes, never gave full confidence to the Western leaders. In a chapter called "Stalin's Ambitions," Hull has related how in the last days of 1941 and again in the spring of 1942, the Russian leaders pressed London to sign a secret treaty which would have promised them large territorial gains. Against this Churchill was adamant. So was the American Government, to which the British promptly transmitted the substance of the Russian proposals. "There is no doubt," Hull and his advisers told Roosevelt, "that the Soviet Government has tremendous ambitions with regard to Europe. . . ." To assent in advance to them would have meant only a temporary improvement in relations with Moscow, would have offended small countries, would have disturbed Latin America and the Vatican, and would have weakened the principles of the Atlantic Charter. The British, supported by the United States, refused to sign anything but a straight public treaty of alliance.

Then in June, 1942, Molotov visited Washington. He arrived under the code name "Mr. Brown," for Stalin had stipulated that the visit be secret. With great insistence, approaching rudeness, Molotov demanded that America and Britain create a second front that year. General Marshall and Admiral King pointed out that this would mean diverting ships from the transport of supplies to Russia. At times Molotov became "gruff," "assertive," and "pressing." After his return home a vague public statement, which he had written, was issued. It declared that a full understanding had been reached with regard to the urgent tasks of creating a second front in Europe in 1942. Actually, however, the conference was followed by what Harry Hopkins's biographer calls "interminable and often violently acrimonious discussion."

Circumstances soon forbade all hope of an offen-

sive in France (the code name was "Sledgehammer") in 1942. Eisenhower has explained that
Churchill was quite right in declaring a direct attack on the Cotentin Peninsula at that stage too
dangerous. The volume and range of fighter aircraft were insufficient. A bloody repulse might have
occurred—and Churchill repeatedly said this was
the one way in which the Allies could really lose
the war. Moreover, the British met disaster at
Tobruk. There seemed a chance that German
troops would capture Alexandria, Cairo, and the
Suez Canal. They might even push east to join
hands with the Japanese forces. An Allied attack
on North Africa ("Torch") was therefore substi-
tuted for "Sledgehammer." While Churchill was its
chief backer, Stimson tells us that it was also
Roosevelt's "great secret baby." Churchill, in token
of the desperate anxiety of British and American
leaders to reassure and cooperate with the Russians, went to Moscow to explain the situation;
and he and Averell Harriman, who accompanied
him as American representative, met a frigid re-
ception. To Harriman the Russian dictator harshly
remarked, "Wars are not won with *plans*." To
Churchill he said that if the British infantry would
only fight the Germans as the Russians (and indeed the R.A.F.) had done, they would not be so
frightened of the foe. Churchill crisply rejoined: "I

pardon that remark only on account of the bravery of the Russian troops." After a time Stalin grew more cordial. He admitted the great advantage of the North African blow: it would take the Germans in the rear, make French and Germans fight each other, put Italy out of the war, and secure Spanish neutrality. On the last evening he and Churchill adjourned to the Kremlin for "some drinks," and talked for seven hours. The Prime Minister cabled Roosevelt that the meetings had ended in great good will. Nevertheless, relations remained precarious.

It was not until the autumn of 1943 that partial diplomatic and strategic cooperation with Russia was achieved. It was high time. Despite the successes already won by American and British forces in clearing the enemy from North Africa, occupying Sicily and Southern Italy, and pressing the Germans up the peninsula; despite the American victories in the Pacific; despite the Anglo–American bombing of Germany, the Russians still complained (with much justice) that they were bearing the brunt of the war. Little had yet been done, they declared, to relieve the German pressure upon them. They were bearing the heavy losses. The British and Americans, meanwhile, were puzzled by the lack of response from the Russians. A hopeful plan had been suggested for basing an Anglo-

American air force in the Caucasus; it was never accepted. Other plans for joint action and strategy were rebuffed.

Secretary Hull undertook to deal with the situation. The tenuous Russian links with the other United Nations had to be strengthened if the war was to be won and the peace safeguarded. Traveling by air to Moscow, the aged Secretary spent nearly a fortnight, October 19–31, in conference with the Russian Foreign Minister, Molotov, the Chinese Foreign Minister, Foo Ping-sheung, and the British Foreign Secretary, Eden. The conversations were unexpectedly harmonious. Hull could point to the large lend-lease shipments, and Eden to the substantial British aid. Both could promise a tremendous Anglo-American invasion of western Europe the following year. Ere the conference broke up, it issued the Moscow Declaration that Russia, Britain, and the United States would fight the war to an unconditional surrender. This, of course, was something gained; yet it did not carry the cooperation of West and East very far. And as the Russian armies continued to move westward, the action of the Soviet Government in the winter of 1943–44 showed that it intended to make itself secure in a definite sphere of influence. While not excluding international cooperation, Russia was pursuing an imperialistic policy in the lands of eastern Europe.

Just before the year 1943 ended, the most important conference yet held brought the heads of the four greatest states into personal touch. Journeying in late November to Cairo, Roosevelt met the Chinese generalissimo, Chiang Kai-shek—of whose character and policy he was decidedly dubious. They talked over plans for war and peace in the Far East, uniting in a declaration that the United States and China would liberate all the occupied areas of the Pacific, and that China would obtain restitution of Manchuria, Formosa, and the Pescadores. Then from Cairo the President and Churchill flew to Tcheran, where they met Stalin for four days of conferences, November 29 to December 1, inclusive. With Roosevelt went a large American group, including Harry Hopkins, Admiral Leahy, and Averell Harriman.

This conference was one of the great events of the war and indeed of modern history. Its principal military object was to coordinate the forthcoming Anglo–American attack on Germany with the Russian movement from the east, and to make sure that Hitler would stagger under simultaneous blows from two fronts. Unfortunately, political considerations complicated the strategic picture. Churchill, who honestly believed that Germany could best be attacked through "the soft under-belly of Europe," wished to see democratic forces in Yugoslavia and Austria when the war ended; Stalin wished to restrict the Anglo-American troops to Western Europe. Time was to prove that much could be said for the advisability of including Anglo-American as well as Russian forces in the occupation of the Balkans. However, purely military considerations pointed to the advisability of a direct cross-channel attack—the "Overlord" on which General Eisenhower insisted. It was agreed that the forces of the English-speaking nations and Russia should carry on a relentless struggle until they met in central Europe. It was also agreed that the United Nations would act together in making an enduring peace. Stalin promised that Russia would fight Japan as soon as the defeat of Germany was accomplished.

To gain Russian cooperation (for some fear existed that the Soviet Union might relax her efforts before reaching Berlin) Roosevelt and Churchill had to make far-reaching promises. In discussing post-war affairs, they conceded to Stalin, in effect if not explicitly, a decisive voice in fixing her future political relations with Poland, Finland, Rumania, Bulgaria, and Hungary; and they thus went far toward establishing that Russian dominance in these areas which was to be so momentous a fact after the war. The Moscow decision to set up a new world organization was confirmed at Teheran. The President defined his ideas. Three main bodies should be created, he said: an Assembly composed of all members of the United Nations; an Executive Committee comprising Russia, the United States, Britain, China, and a number of other countries; and a police force supported by the four great powers. It was significant that Stalin objected to the police agency, saying that small nations would not like it. A prolonged discussion of the future of Germany also took place. Roosevelt offered a plan for dividing the country into five autonomous states; though Churchill seemed willing to accept this with some amendments, Stalin objected to the scheme. Finally, the three leaders signed a declaration on Iran, pledging careful consideration of her economic needs when peace came, and affirming their desire to see her sovereignty and territorial integrity respected.

At Teheran some discussion of the policy of demanding unconditional surrender took place. Roosevelt had first announced this in his casual way, to the amazement of Churchill, at a press conference during the Casablanca meeting (January, 1943). It had staggered Secretary Hull, who had not been consulted, and who desired more flexible terms of surrender. Critics in America and England at once pointed out that the demand for unconditional surrender would prolong the war by causing Germany and Japan to fight desperately to the end; and evidence exists that it did discourage internal resistance to the Governments in these countries. They also pointed out that it implied that the victors must be ready to take over every phase of administration in the conquered lands; as they ultimately did in both Germany and Japan. Of course much could be said for the principle, but there was reason to believe that it had been reached too hastily. In the Teheran discussion the British said they much preferred a simple demand for "prompt surrender," and the Russians also expressed grave doubts. As a result, President Roosevelt on Christmas Eve of 1943 delivered a radio address in which he declared that the United Nations had no wish to enslave the German people, but hoped to see them develop in peace as useful and respectable members of the European family. This was a much-needed modification of an excessively sweeping principle.

For the purposes of waging war, the alliance of America, the British Commonwealth, China, and Russia was now seemingly complete. Nevertheless, behind the imposing outer façade of unity, the antagonisms of developing power politics were already visible. Robert E. Sherwood, in *Roosevelt and Hopkins,* has revealed details of another of the crises of these times. When Stalin received plans for the invasion of France that fixed D-Day in June, 1944, he became angry and sent Churchill a cablegram reviewing the assurances of help during the previous thirteen months and concluding with words that amounted to a charge of deliberate bad faith on the part of America and Britain. The incensed Churchill responded with a scorching message. A period of tension ensued. Stalin recalled Ambassador Litvinov from Washington and Ambassador Maisky from London. The atmosphere, writes Sherwood, became alarmingly reminiscent of that which had surrounded the Molotov-Ribbentrop Pact. "It was fortunate that Hitler did not know how bad the relations were between the Allies at that moment, how close they were to the disruption which was his only hope of survival." But that these thoroughly embattled nations would hang together until Hitler, Mussolini, and the Japanese militarists were utterly vanquished there could be little doubt.

CHAPTER X

As in 1942–43 the war became more desperate, as additional nations joined the front against Germany and Japan, and as the Anglo-American forces, after conquering North Africa, turned to Italy, the foreign relations of the United States grew dismayingly complex. Throughout half the world fresh difficulties had to be faced.

It was gratifying that within nine months after Pearl Harbor eleven Latin-American nations (the Caribbean and Central American republics, with Mexico and Brazil) declared war against the Axis. But while they loyally aided the war effort, they had to be given support in various ways. Meanwhile, Argentina was a focus of concern, for it was ruled by a military regime which (as the State Department shortly charged) was openly and notoriously giving "affirmative assistance to the declared enemies of the United Nations." The invasion of North Africa brought relations with Spain to a crisis. Her dictator Franco had declared that American intervention in the war was criminal madness, and had asserted that if Berlin were ever in peril a million Spaniards would help protect it; he had to be kept quiet and his covert aid to Hitler suppressed. Relations with the sorry Government maintained by Marshal Pétain at Vichy for unoccupied France had always been difficult. They became impossible when the Anglo-American expedition invaded North Africa, for Pétain broke off diplomatic contacts, while Hitler instantly seized the remainder of French home territory. What leader should America now support as the symbol of French liberation? In still other areas painful diplomatic problems arose to vex President Roosevelt and Secretary Hull.

Of all these problems, those of Spain and France generated the most heat at home and abroad. In dealing with Madrid, the American and British Governments had the task of intimidating Franco, and yet keeping their pressure below the point which would drive him into open alliance with Hitler and Mussolini. They had no illusions as to his hostility. Spain supplied German industry with wolfram and other vital materials, it sent a volunteer Blue Division to fight Russia, and it fixed a price for opening hostilities on the Axis side, Franco demanding Gibraltar, French Morocco, and other territorial accessions. Yet the impoverished country seethed with discontent, and large elements sympathized with the democracies.

The two active agents in holding Spain in check were Sir Samuel Hoare and Carlton J. H. Hayes as British and American Ambassadors in Madrid. To a great degree Spain was a German-occupied country; a saying was current that Hitler could take it by telephone. But as the poverty, exhaustion, and discontent of the nation forbade it to wage war for more than a few months, Franco wished to enter the conflict just before the end. In the first phase of their work, the two Ambassadors cut down the flow of supplies to Germany by preclusive buying, hammered Franco with protests and threats, carried on intelligence activities, and conducted vigorous Allied propaganda. In the second phase, they made sure that Spanish forces would not interfere with the African landings, and that Gibraltar would be an active naval and air base for the Anglo-American armies. Both Hoare and Hayes were harassed by leftist attacks at home on their policies. Yet they ably achieved their aims.

The Anglo-American "bribery" in offering Spain credits, shipping facilities, wheat, and petroleum was accompanied by skillful negotiations for equivalents. As the democracies gained military successes, they heightened their pressure. The Embassies kept in touch with Franco's opponents, and built up the popular antagonism to war. When North Africa was invaded, Eisenhower kept a large force ready to meet any flank attack by Franco's Moroccan troops; when the Germans were cleared out of Tunis, a sterner tone was adopted. A temporary embargo on oil forced Spain to cut down wolfram exports to the Nazis. Because the Allies shut off Spanish wool from Germany, many of Hitler's soldiers froze to death in the Russian snows. In time Franco was compelled to recall his Blue Division from Germany. Before the war ended, he had changed his quasi-belligerency on the Axis side to a neutrality favorable to the United Nations.

Though America and Britain acted together in Spain, they followed divergent lines in dealing with France. The British in 1940–41 adopted a policy of cordial cooperation with the Free French regime of General Charles de Gaulle. They accepted a rupture of relations with Pétain, demanded the surrender or destruction of Vichy warships, joined Free French forces in attacking the Vichy garrison at Dakar, conquered Vichy-controlled Syria and Madagascar, and helped De Gaulle to take over French Equatorial Africa. These acts were an indispensable part of their war against the Axis. At the same time, London refrained from giving full recognition to the De Gaulle regime.*

The United States meanwhile maintained diplomatic relations with Vichy in an effort to strengthen Pétain in resisting German demands. Washington hoped in this way to lessen collaboration with the Germans, keep the French fleet ("perhaps the biggest single stake in the whole business," according

* The course of events in prostrate France was too complicated to be summarized in full. Following the action of the British fleet on July 3, 1940, to destroy French naval units at Oran, Dakar, and Mers-el-Kebir lest they fall into German hands, the Pétain Government broke off diplomatic relations with Britain and accepted German vassalage. Pétain was proclaimed chief of state or dictator, with power to recast the constitution. Three former premiers, Blum, Daladier, and Reynaud, were arrested for trial on charges of war guilt. In December, 1940, Pétain, believing that Vice-Premier Pierre Laval was intriguing to bring about full German control, dismissed the man and had him arrested. For several months his place as second in command was taken by Admiral François Darlan, who believed in full cooperation with the Germans. Darlan acted in close partnership with the Nazi officials, aided them in an attempt to take control of Syria, and would have let them make use of the African ports of Bizerte and Dakar had not General Maxime Weygand interfered. In April, 1942, Laval was brought back to the second position in the French Government, while Darlan was made Commander-in-Chief of French forces. Meanwhile, General Charles de Gaulle, who before the war had insisted that French defense should be based on reorganized mobile forces instead of on the Maginot Line, had gone to England and in 1940 built up the Free French resistance movement to real strength. By July, 1942, he had an army of about a hundred thousand volunteers, rechristened "Fighting France." Naturally the most bitter hatred existed between De Gaulle and Pétain. The Pétain regime excused its consent to the occupation of Southern Indo-China on the ground that if Japan did not move in, De Gaulle and the British would.

to W. L. Langer) out of Nazi hands, and maintain North Africa free from German controls. The situation in 1941 was touch and go. While Pétain retained some vestiges of his backbone, Admiral Darlan, head of the fleet, was a rank collaborationist with Germany. Many of the upper classes in France leaned toward collaboration while the lower classes tended to admire De Gaulle. A considerable section of the banking and manufacturing interests were ready to assist the Nazis. Fascism had taken a deep hold upon France, many ministers and subordinate officials were tools of the Germans, and Pierre Pucheu organized a French secret police as ruthless as the Nazi Gestapo. Under these circumstances, many Americans angrily condemned the good relations of Washington with the Vichy Government. They declared that the United States was supporting traitors to France and tools of the Germans. The British were disgusted with the economic aid which America gave to Vichy North Africa at a time when the Nazis were notoriously draining materials from that region. During 1941, in fact, about five million tons of foodstuffs, valuable ores, and other goods were taken out of North Africa, of which from three-fifths to four-fifths went to Germany. Nevertheless, the American policy had great benefits.

This policy enabled the Ambassador to Vichy, Admiral William D. Leahy, to stiffen Pétain against

Darlan, to encourage the French in resistance, to protect refugees, and to obtain valuable information. Above all, he could make preparations which smoothed the path for the African invasion. He was assisted by Robert Murphy, Roosevelt's personal representative in French North Africa in 1940–42. Murphy established friendly relations with General Maxime Weygand, administrative chief in North Africa, who was loyal to Pétain but hoped for German defeat. Under the Murphy-Weygand Agreement early in 1941 the United States furnished North Africa with much-needed American supplies on condition that they be consumed exclusively in that area, and that American officials control their handling in North African ports and on the railroads. This did something to check German infiltration and enabled Americans to observe conditions. Weygand did his utmost to keep Germans out of his domain and to discourage collaboration with them. Murphy, establishing an office in Algiers to supervise the control organization, built up a vigilant staff. He and his agents did much to prepare the ground for the impending invasion.

Then occurred a dramatic series of events. In the summer of 1942, American officers established relations with General Henri Giraud, who had escaped from the German fortress of Königstein in April, and who was anxious for a United Nations victory. Protracted negotiations with this blunt, honest, obstinate, none-too-intelligent soldier ensued. They reached their climax when Eisenhower had Giraud brought by submarine and flying boat to Gibraltar. The Frenchman, "a gallant if bedraggled figure," talked with great fighting spirit. He labored under the misapprehension that he was to be Commander-in-Chief of the Allied invasion of Africa! At first he refused to cooperate; he could not be a subordinate. Then, on the very eve of the invasion, an agreement was reached. Giraud was to support the operation, try to stop French resistance, and be made French commander and governor in North Africa.

The diplomatic maneuvers which resulted in this last-minute agreement caused confusion and irritation in the United States. Nor were the results wholly happy. When the Anglo-American troops landed (November 7, 1942) they met hot French resistance. The "honor" of the Vichy regime was salved by the totally unnecessary killing of many Americans, Britons, and Frenchmen. When Giraud ordered the Vichy forces to cease fire he got no response. And at that critical moment one of the worst of the collaborationists entered the scene. Admiral Darlan had arrived in North Africa to visit a paralyzed son just before the invasion. A Fascist reactionary, a traitor, and an Anglophobe, he was detested by Churchill, Roosevelt, and De

Gaulle. But he was pliable and he could be used. Murphy, active in Algiers, told him the invasion was starting, held him in parley until it was under way, and so convinced him of its strength and probability of success that he changed sides and agreed to do business with the Allies. Eisenhower accepted his help. His first attempt to get General Noguès's army in Morocco to stop fighting Patton's troops failed. But later on Darlan did better. He persuaded the French to drop their resistance, and thus saved precious hours as well as lives. He brought about the surrender of naval units to the Allies; he induced the Dakar command to give up that valuable port. Yet he continued to play a double part, ready to rejoin the Nazis if they proved the stronger.

A wave of protest and denunciation against Darlan's aid rose all over the world: in Russia, in Britain, in De Gaullist circles in France, and not least in America, where Wendell Willkie led a chorus of liberal dismay. President Roosevelt had to explain that the arrangement with the man was "only a temporary expedient, justified solely by the stress of battle." At the same time he informed Eisenhower that the American Government did not trust Darlan, wanted him watched carefully, and wished him removed from power as soon as possible. The assassination of the Frenchman on December 24 caused general relief. Whether the material benefits of partial cooperation with Vichy and Darlan outweighed the moral damages will always be a debatable issue. The weight of opinion, with Hull, Marshall, and Eisenhower concurring, is that the policy was justified by results.

Relations with the French remained complicated and painful. As Pétain and Laval (a worse traitor than Darlan) became mere tools of the Nazis, now occupying all France, it was clear that the true hope of the nation lay in De Gaulle's Free French movement. Powerful groups in the United States insisted that the tall, temperamental, and egotistical general be accepted as provisional leader of France. Roosevelt and Churchill found much in his personality to irritate them. "My worst cross is the Cross of Lorraine!" sighed Churchill—that being De Gaulle's symbol. Roosevelt told the doubtful story that at Casablanca De Gaulle had announced theatrically: "I am Joan of Arc! I am Clemenceau!" Yet he gained ground. First the Allies supported a Committee of National Liberation, erected at Algiers in June, 1943, of which De Gaulle and Giraud were joint presidents. Then some two months later America, Britain, and Russia gave limited recognition to De Gaulle. The energy of his activities brought many Frenchmen to his standard, and in the fall of 1944 his committee was recognized as the Provisional Government of the republic. It did much, in the crucial days thereafter, to strengthen the resistance movement in France, and to help prepare for the cross-Channel invasion.

This great invasion, termed "Overlord" by those planning it, inevitably involved diplomatic considerations. The general belief in Allied circles prior to the Quebec Conference had been that the supreme commander would be a Briton. But when it became plain that an overwhelming preponderance of troops used would be Americans, Churchill cordially agreed with Roosevelt that an American leader should be appointed. For a time it was uncertain whether the commander would be Marshall or Eisenhower. A definite indication of preference by Churchill would have decided the matter. He left it to Roosevelt, who after much hesitation decided that Marshall should remain Chief of Staff while Eisenhower took charge of "Overlord." The logical ground for this was that Eisenhower was familiar with the European theatre, while Marshall had a grasp of the war as a world-wide conflict; it would take each man months to learn his new task if Marshall took a field command while Eisenhower assumed staff leadership. Chief place under Eisenhower as commander of ground forces went to the brilliant Sir Bernard Montgomery, while another able Briton, General Sir Harold Alexander, retained the Italian command. The concentration of effort upon the invasion of France meant the shelving of Churchill's long-cherished plan for a heavy stroke in the Balkan area. It meant equally the shelving of two strong operations in Southeast Asia on which Roosevelt had given definite promises to Chiang Kai-shek, promises which he revoked in December, 1943, at the time of the Teheran Conference.

The decisions at Teheran involved other nations than the chief powers and Iran. With the Turkish President and Foreign Minister present, discussions were held on the possibility of bringing Turkey into the war. This was much desired by Churchill and Stalin, and favored more skeptically by Roosevelt. The American Chiefs of Staff regarded it with disfavor as certain to "burn up our logistics right down the line." Turkey refused to move until made so strong that all danger of conquest by Germany could be written off; in the end, she did not move at all. An inconclusive discussion was also held at Teheran on means of getting Finland out of her wartime alliance with Germany. Talks took place on post-war questions: the Polish boundaries, the division of the Italian fleet, and above all the treatment of Germany, which Roosevelt proposed should be made a federation of five self-governing states. The principal decisions, however, apart from "Overlord" and the coordination of the final Russian effort with the Anglo-American invasion, were those taken against military adventures in the Balkans and eastern Mediterranean, and against a costly new involvement of force in Southeast Asia.

The situation in China offered the Allies one discouragement after another. Repeated efforts by American representatives to settle the bloody quarrel between the Kuomintang Government of Chiang Kai-shek and the Communists came to nothing. Both sides desired the unification of China, but they asserted principles that were irreconcilable. By the closing years of the war the Communists, well entrenched in north central China with their capital in Shensi Province, laid claim to a civilian population of nearly 100,000,-000. Their army was more poorly equipped than Chiang's, but about as strong in numbers and superior in spirit. While they professed adherence to Marxist ideas and expressed strong sympathy for Russia, they struck observers as primarily Chinese nationalists independent of foreign control. Their principles of land-tenure reform, promotion of scientific agriculture, and honest tax administration possessed great merit. The United States recognized only the Kuomintang Government, which it gave steady moral and material support. But many American representatives, including Ambassador Patrick Hurley, were highly critical of Chiang's policies and of the corruption and inefficiency of the Kuomintang administration. Difficulties between Chiang and the peppery

American commander in the Burma area, General Joseph W. Stilwell, culminated in Chiang's demand for the General's dismissal. Financial and economic disorder in China grew steadily worse.

As the war entered its final phase, Chiang's Government demanded that the Communist armies and administration acknowledge the supreme authority of the Kuomintang. The Communists, for their part, demanded a new coalition government of both great factions and of smaller parties, based upon universal suffrage and uncontrolled elections. Both major parties were eager to occupy the vital districts held by the Japanese. Meanwhile, although the Soviet Government had concluded an alliance with the Chiang regime and had engaged not to meddle in China's internal affairs, the shadow of Russia fell across all Manchuria.

An equal source of exasperation was found in Argentina. That country, though small in population, was important because the world urgently needed its wheat and beef, and because it could make or break the unity of Latin America. Its policy was exasperating because for a number of reasons (dislike of the "materialistic" and "imperialistic" United States, jealousy of "Negroid" Brazil, irritation over a stationary population and stagnant economy, a desire for self-assertion and leadership, a hope to bet on victorious world forces), powerful groups accepted Fascist ideas

and the Axis propaganda. Much of the Argentine
population, with a tradition of the dictator, took
naturally to the idea of a *Caudillo* or strong leader.
Not a few military-minded people hoped that
Uruguay, Paraguay, and other lost provinces, with
the British-held Falklands, might be brought under
the sway of Buenos Aires. Hitler's ideas of *Lebensraum* therefore had a wide appeal. A series of
chieftains, beginning with Castillo and ending
with Farrell, believed that the Axis might well
triumph in Europe, and that Argentina could reap
a golden harvest from partnership with the triumphant dictators. As Dr. Frank Tannenbaum
wrote in *Foreign Affairs* (July, 1945): "The repudiation of solemnly accepted international commitments, the contemptuous suppression of constitutional procedure, the jailing and exiling of
opponents and critics, the harboring of German
spies, the resuscitation of Rosas as the great national hero, all the wild talk and action, is meant
to 'save' the nation. Save it from what? From a
delusion of encirclement, a delusion half-believed
and half-fostered for a purpose—the purpose of re-
establishing the greater Argentina."

If the Axis had won the war, Argentina would
have embarked on a policy of expansion. Supported by Germany, herself eager for footholds in
Latin America, the dictatorship in Buenos Aires
would have looked for territorial gains north, east,

and west; and, if the Antarctic be added, in the
south as well. Realization of this fact, dislike of
Fascist tendencies within Argentina, and resentment over the disruption of the common Pan-
American front made Secretary Hull sternly hostile toward the Argentine Government. His hand
was restrained, however, by several considerations.
For one, Latin-American sentiment was more
tolerant of the dictators in Buenos Aires than was
Washington. For another, Great Britain set a high
value on Argentine foodstuffs, remembered her
long and successful economic partnership with Argentina, and thought of her investments in that
country. For a third reason, it was possible that a
sudden overthrow of the military leadership in Argentina might give dangerous encouragement to
Communist elements in Latin America.

The overthrow of Pedro Ramirez by a military
clique and the installation of General Edelmiro
Farrell in his stead (March 10, 1944) brought the
situation to a crisis. Ramirez had finally broken
diplomatic relations with the Axis. The Farrell
Government was supported by men (one of them
a Fascist-minded colonel named Juan Domingo
Perón) friendly to the Nazis and hostile to the
United States. It soon became plain that it was
carrying out an unfriendly policy. As Hull has
written, the Farrell regime freed Axis spies and
agents previously arrested, gave Axis diplomats

full rein throughout the country, supported a group of pro-Axis newspapers, withheld critical materials from firms friendly to the Allies, and awarded large official contracts to Axis firms. It set up a Fascist dictatorship, controlling schools, muzzling the press, putting the courts in a strait-jacket, and trampling down fundamental civil rights. Bad as the Castillo and Ramirez administrations had been, that of Farrell was worse. In midsummer of 1944, Roosevelt and Hull exploded in an emphatic public statement, accusing Argentina of deliberately violating her pledge to the other American republics, and of taking steps which had gravely injured the Allied cause. As yet no American republic save Bolivia had recognized the Farrell Government. The President and Secretary urged continuance of this non-recognition until Argentina changed her course. Argentine stocks of gold in Washington were frozen, and American ships were forbidden to enter Argentine ports. The British Government acted firmly with the United States.

So matters stood when, as the war approached its end, it became important that the Latin-American nations make a concerted effort to meet its final issues. Beginning February 21, 1945, the Inter-American Conference on Problems of War and Peace met in Chapultepec Castle, near Mexico City, scene of the gallant defense by the Mexican cadets against the invading Americans under Winfield Scott. At this gathering Argentina was of course not represented. The most cordial unity prevailed. All the capitals of the New World save Buenos Aires were anxious to unify and strengthen their martial effort and to agree upon the principles of post-war solidarity in the Western Hemisphere. They proscribed territorial conquest; they reiterated their condemnation of intervention in the internal or external affairs of another state; they declared again for the settlement of inter-American disputes by conciliation, adjudication, or unrestricted arbitration. Above all, they took a momentous forward step in making the Monroe Doctrine a multilateral instead of a unilateral arrangement. The nations represented agreed to join in guardianship of the principles of the Doctrine, treating any attempt against the integrity, independence, sovereignty, or inviolability of one American state as an act of aggression against all of them. All this was embodied in the Act of Chapultepec.

As for Argentina, notice was served upon her that only if she accepted the Act and came into the war against the Axis would she be admitted to the United Nations. The Conference broke up on March 8. Less than twenty days later, Argentina ratified the Act and opened hostilities upon Germany and Japan. Nevertheless, difficulties with

Buenos Aires continued. Early in 1946, through a Presidential election attended by certain "irregularities," the Farrell-Perón regime was replaced by a full Perón dictatorship. A few weeks later the State Department, which had already brought out a Blue Book on Argentine relations, issued a troubled memorandum to the other American republics. Buenos Aires was still on trial, it stated in effect. "The policy of non-intervention in internal affairs does not mean the approval of local tyranny."

By the time of the Act of Chapultepec, with victory in Europe and the Pacific in full sight, Secretary Hull had finished his long labors for the cause of world order. Stricken by illness, he resigned November 30, 1944, and was succeeded by Under Secretary Edward R. Stettinius. As we have seen, some sides of foreign policy (and during the war the most important sides) were Roosevelt's peculiar province. But other sides had been Hull's own care, and his work for the reduction of tariffs, the liberation of world trade, the strengthening of the good neighbor policy with Latin America, the deepening of our indispensable friendship with the British Commonwealth, and the revival of the Wilsonian idea of collective security, gave him a place among the greatest of American Secretaries of State.

CHAPTER XI

THE NEW WORLD ORDER

ONE bright vision, during all these years of storm and wreck, had never died from the gaze of millions of plain folk the world over. "If the League of Nations has been mishandled and broken," said Churchill in Manchester in May, 1938, "we must rebuild it. If a League of peace-seeking peoples is set at naught, we must convert it into a League of armed peoples, too faithful to molest others, too strong to be molested themselves."

During the First World War too little thought had been given to peace while the cannon spoke. Many leaders of the democracies, many organizations for peace, were resolved that this error should not be repeated. At an early date united effort began. The very name of the United Nations implied a pledge for world organization. In the spring of 1943 the member countries, then forty-four in number, took their first notable step in concert by holding a conference on food at Hot Springs, Virginia. From the discussions emerged plans for several important world undertakings.

The delegates agreed on the creation of the Food and Agriculture Organization of the United Nations, charged with helping member countries produce and distribute food with more efficiency. They agreed that a United Nations trade conference was needed. They discovered that agreements for sharing such commodities as wheat, cotton, and sugar would be essential. They pointed out that a conference on international monetary policies, already planned, would greatly assist in food distribution. Most important of all, the obvious necessity for post-war relief on a grand scale led to plans for setting up the United Nations Relief and Rehabilitation Administration, soon famous as UNRRA.

Meanwhile, discussion of a new and more efficient world organization had begun. Secretary Hull had been talking of it with his associates in the State Department, and during the summer of 1943 they drafted a Four-Nation Declaration, under which America, Britain, Russia, and China would agree to establish at the earliest practicable date an organization, open to all countries, for the maintenance of international peace and security. At the Quebec Conference in August, Hull showed this to Churchill and Anthony Eden, who warmly approved it, and suggested sending it to Moscow for an opinion by Stalin and Molotov. The first response of Russia was chilly. The Soviet Government rejected the Declaration. Hull was heartened, however, by passage in the House of the Fulbright Resolution, introduced by Representative J. W. Fulbright, of Arkansas. This put the lower chamber on record as favoring the creation of a world organization, the United States participating, with power adequate to maintain lasting peace among the nations. A conference of Republican leaders at Mackinac, in which Will H. Hays was active, committed itself to such action. Early in November the Senate by an overwhelming majority voted the Connally Resolution, urging that the United States join with other sovereign nations in establishing and maintaining an international authority with power to prevent aggression and preserve world peace. This represented a revolution in opinion since the days of isolationist ascendancy in the mid-thirties.

Nor did Soviet Russia long continue reluctant. When Secretary Hull, boarding an airplane for the first time in his life, flew to the meeting of Foreign Ministers in Moscow in October, 1943, he was above all else anxious to obtain a commitment to a world organization. Amid much vodka drinking by subordinates, he pointed out to Stalin that isolationism had almost ruined both their countries, and Stalin heartily agreed. The Four-Power

Declaration was accepted. Hull returned in high elation to make his report to an enthusiastic Congress—the first time that a Secretary of State had addressed a joint session. The dominant thought of the conference, he said, "was that, after the attainment of victory, cooperation among peace-loving nations in support of certain paramount mutual interests will be almost as compelling in importance and necessity as it is today in support of the war effort."

During this same summer and fall a draft plan for UNRRA was hammered out in Washington. Already the ravages of war had plunged tens of millions into utter destitution, so that an unprecedented world effort would be needed to succor starving and naked populations. After signing the draft agreement which set up UNRRA under a Director-General and Council (November 9, 1943), delegates proceeded to Atlantic City. Here they devised machinery for carrying out the relief work, fixed on approximately two billion dollars as the initial sum needed, and accepted the principle that each member-nation should contribute one per cent of its income for the fiscal year 1942–43. This made the initial American contribution $1,350,000,000. So far as possible, needy peoples were to be assisted to help themselves. Though rehabilitation was not to include reconstruction (a job left for later organizations), UNRRA did accept partial responsibility for the work of repatriating the vast multitudes of displaced persons. Ex-Governor Herbert H. Lehman of New York became the first head, and was later succeeded by the explosive Fiorello La Guardia. They were capable, and with help, notably from a British administrator, General Frederick Morgan, the organization did a magnificent piece of work.

Nothing was more remarkable than the almost complete collapse of isolationism in its historic citadel, the Senate. If the Connally resolution and the ovation to Hull on his return from Moscow showed that, so did the bipartisan approach to world problems. Four members, Joseph H. Ball, Harold H. Burton, Carl A. Hatch, and Lister Hill, representing both parties, had made a special effort to educate their associates. Hull talked with them and with members of the Foreign Relations Committee. The old friendships of the Secretary in both chambers were an asset of incalculable value. In the spring of 1944 he persuaded the Senate leaders to appoint a bipartisan committee of eight to confer regularly with the President and State Department on foreign affairs, thus forestalling the growth of jealousy or suspicion in the Senate. The errors made by Woodrow Wilson were not to be repeated—but then, tempers had changed since Wilson's time.

The country entered the Presidential campaign

of 1944 with almost flawless unity upon the main
foreign problems. At an early date the experienced
Breckinridge Long, a moderate Wilsonian Demo-
crat now Assistant Secretary of State, began
laboring quietly to induce both parties to accept
platform planks favoring a world organization.
On the Republican side he received vigorous assistance from Secretaries Stimson and Knox, Will H.
Hays, Myron Taylor (former Chairman of the
United States Steel Corporation, now unofficial
representative of President Roosevelt at the Vatican), and leading Senators. The desired planks
were adopted by both Republicans and Democrats.
Thomas E. Dewey, nominated by the Republicans,
had belatedly but firmly committed himself to
world organization. Though he assailed the Administration's course in foreign affairs as secret and
erratic, in a speech at Louisville he condemned the
isolationism of Hamilton Fish and Hiram Johnson. Roosevelt, renominated by the Democrats
with Harry S. Truman as candidate for Vice-President, emphasized the importance of international
cooperation, and declared that the American delegates on the proposed Security Council should be
empowered in advance to use American troops in
a world crisis. When Dewey refused to go that far,
Senator Ball of Minnesota bolted his party to join
Roosevelt.

The President's reelection by a popular vote of

25,611,000 to 22,018,000, and 432 electoral votes to 99, was in part a ringing endorsement of his international policies. It was accompanied by the defeat of prominent isolationists in Congress, including Senator Gerald Nye, of munitions-inquiry fame, and Representative Hamilton Fish.

A reminder that the labor problem now had to be dealt with on an international plane had immediately preceded the election of 1944; a heroic effort to deal with the complex problems of international exchange and international credits accompanied it. The International Labor Organization, a part of the League which had found refuge during the war in Montreal, obviously had to be carried over into the new world organization. Holding its twenty-sixth session in Philadelphia in the spring of 1944, the I.L.O. discussed minimum labor standards, full employment, the treatment of labor in colonial areas, and the future of German trade unions. On May 10 it adopted the "Philadelphia Charter," a declaration of basic aims and purposes. The most important parts of this document, signed by more than forty nations, were that labor is not a commodity; that poverty anywhere is a menace to prosperity everywhere; that security and opportunity must be promoted without respect to race, creed, or sex; and that all nations must strive for full employment and the elevation of standards of living.

This was a contribution to the economic peace of the post-war world; and a still more ambitious contribution to the same end was made by the United Nations Monetary and Financial Conference held amid the picturesque mountain scenery of Bretton Woods, New Hampshire. In 1942 two elaborate plans, one drafted by Lord Keynes and the other by Harry D. White of the Treasury Department, were published. They served as a basis for discussion; after much revision, they were united in a compromise plan (April, 1944), and the United States then invited forty-three nations to send representatives to Bretton Woods. With more than four hundred delegates present and Secretary Henry Morgenthau, Jr., presiding, the conference opened in July. White and Keynes directed the two commissions which did most of the work, and a far-reaching agreement was finally signed.

The core of this agreement lay in the creation of an International Monetary Fund and a World Bank to meet two different needs. The Fund, initially set at $8,800,000,000, to be contributed by member-nations according to fixed quotas, was created primarily to see that the currencies of the world were exchanged at a nearly constant rate. It was also devised to cushion members against temporary dislocations in foreign trade. When such shocks occurred, the nations could buy from the Fund such foreign currencies as they needed, paying in their own money. Each nation agreed not to alter the par value of its currency except after consulting with the Fund and in harmony with certain basic rules. Equally important was the International Bank for Reconstruction and Development, which was given a potential capital of $10,000,000,000. It was set up to make loans to member-nations for projects which private banking interests would not support, however needed, and which an expert investigation proved economically sound. Obviously, at the war's close many impoverished nations, faced with the rebuilding of cities, port facilities, and industries, would need help that ordinary banks could not give. Only a great international institution could furnish the sums needed to bring these nations back to prosperity and security.

The American contribution to both Fund and Bank was necessarily large, for not only was the United States the most heavily industrialized nation, but it held approximately twenty billions of the world's gold, or well over half. The American quota for the Fund was $2,750,000,000; that for the Bank $1,200,000,000. Heavy opposition came from banking interests which feared that they would suffer from Government interference and competition. But Secretary Morgenthau hailed the agreement as "the most vital step in the path of realizing effective international economic cooperation"; and after a brisk battle, Congress gave its ratification.

While Bretton Woods was dealing with economic peace and stability, representatives of the four chief powers, on the invitation of the United States, met at Dumbarton Oaks in Washington on August 21, 1944, to begin work on a new international charter. On October 7, just as American troops were attacking Aachen in Germany and British fighters were freeing the port of Antwerp, the Dumbarton Oaks Proposals were completed. "There should be established," they began, "an international organization under the title of the United Nations." This organization was to be based on the sovereign equality of peace-loving states, and all such states were to be eligible to membership so that they might "take collective measures for the prevention and removal of threats to the peace" of the globe.

In form, the scheme for the United Nations closely followed the League; the new body was to have an assembly, a council, an international court, and a secretariat. Its General Assembly was to comprise all member-states; its Security Council was to be made up of five great powers with permanent seats, and six rotating nations with non-permanent seats. But the proposals went beyond the old League in several vital respects. They pro-

vided for armed forces directed by a Military Staff
Committee, a police agency with which the Security
Council might discipline aggressive nations. The
Dumbarton Oaks delegates also devised an important new body, the Economic and Social
Council, which it was hoped might in the long run
(as world peace became assured) become the most
important part of the United Nations Organization. These proposals were to be placed before a
general gathering of the United Nations for final
reshaping.

Shortly after the Dumbarton Oaks plan had been
laid before the world, the most important of the
wartime conferences of the Allied leaders took place
at Yalta (February 4–11, 1945). It was the last
conference of the major Allied leaders, Roosevelt,
Churchill, and Stalin; it was by far the most controversial of these gatherings in its results. Accompanied by General Marshall, James F. Byrnes,
Averell Harriman, Harry Hopkins, and other
skilled advisers, the President met the European
leaders in the old Livadia Palace of the Czars. On
the military side the gathering was an unquestioned
success. It put an end to the last German hopes
of dividing the Allies; it perfected plans for the
final stages of the war in Europe; and it reached a
secret agreement by which Russia pledged herself
to enter the war against Japan within two or three
months after the European conflict ended. On the

political side, however, the Yalta bargains shortly generated the sharpest Anglo-American criticism.

The war situation at the time promised much further heavy fighting. On the Western front the Anglo-American forces, having lately recovered the ground lost in the Battle of the Bulge, were just inside the German boundary. In Italy they had made slow progress in the Apennines and still had to reach the Po. In the Far East the American Navy had put the last important Japanese naval forces out of action in the Leyte Gulf; but Luzon still had to be fully conquered, and Iwo Jima and Okinawa still had to be fought. Nobody knew how many months of war would be needed to defeat the Japanese armies in their home islands; how many months to blast the Japanese forces out of the Asiatic mainland. Roosevelt, who was now a sicker man than he knew, but whose intellect according to Hopkins and others was unimpaired, felt himself unable to take a position of strong table-banging defiance toward the Russians. For that matter, he did not want to take such a position. He still believed in the possibility of harmonious cooperation with the Soviet Union. At one point he quoted to Stalin the clause in the Teheran Declaration which had stated: "We recognize fully the supreme responsibility resting upon us and all the nations to make a peace which will command good will from the overwhelming masses

of the peoples of the world." He therefore made
concessions which he expected Russia to use in a
spirit of fairness and good will. He could not foresee that Moscow would violate the spirit (and
sometimes the letter) of the Yalta agreements.

In order to obtain a pledge of Russian aid against
Japan, Roosevelt agreed that the Kurile Islands
and southern Sakhalin should be ceded to the
Soviet Union. He agreed to recognize the dominant
Russian influence in Outer Mongolia. He agreed to
an acceptance of Soviet interests as paramount in
Port Arthur and the Manchurian railways. He
agreed to the Russian occupation of that part of
Korea north of the 38th parallel. All of these concessions were temporarily kept secret; and Roosevelt himself confessed to Byrnes that some ought
not to have been made except in a general treaty
of peace, and with full Chinese consent. The railway stipulations and the lease of Port Arthur to
Russia as a naval base were particularly dubious,
for they seemed to render impossible the exercise
of full Chinese sovereignty in the rich province
of Manchuria. On the insistence of Stalin, these
arrangements were reduced to writing, and were
double-riveted by the statement: "The heads of
the three great Powers have agreed that these
claims of the Soviet Union shall be unquestionably
fulfilled after Japan has been defeated." Roosevelt intended to send an envoy to Chiang Kai-shek

to break the news of the concessions to him and to
win his consent—as soon as Russian troop move-
ments to the Far East had been completed, and the
need for secrecy was ended.

In another secret commitment at Yalta, Roosevelt agreed to support a Russian demand for three
votes instead of one in the United Nations Assembly: one for Russia proper, one for the Ukraine,
and one for Byelorussia or White Russia. Stalin
for his part agreed to support a demand for two
extra American votes if Congress insisted upon it.
Further agreements were reached on the zones of
the major Allies in Germany. This scheme of zonal
occupation had been discussed at Teheran and
worked out in some detail by a European Advisory Commission sitting in London; it was now
decided, at the instance of Churchill and Eden,
that a French zone might be carved out of the
Anglo-American domain. The Russians claimed
very large reparations in kind from the Germans,
mentioning a figure of ten billion dollars; but the
British and Americans objected both to the mode
of payment and the sum, and the question was
postponed.

Considerable discussion took place on the question of the veto in the United Nations Council.
Here, too, a compromise was reached. America and
Britain yielded to Russia's demand that a major
power might veto substantive action by the Coun-

cil (investigation, sanctions, or war) against that power; Russia yielded to the Anglo-American insistence that the Council might consider the position of any power in a dispute, and thereby bring it before the bar of world opinion.

Vague discussions were held, too, and vague understandings reached, on the position of various western Slav nations. Roosevelt and Churchill consented that a line approximating the old Curzon Line should be fixed as the western border of Russia, thus giving the Soviet Union a large area of pre-war Polish territory. In return, Poland was to have substantial accessions of territory in the north and east, the final limits to be fixed by a peace conference. The regime of the pro-Communist Tito in Yugoslovia was granted a large degree of recognition at the expense of the anti-Communist Mikhailovitch. On the other hand, Roosevelt and Churchill obtained from Stalin a promise that parts of eastern Europe overrun by Soviet armies in defeating the Axis would be restored as independent democratic nations. They also obtained assurance that provisional governments in these countries would represent all democratic parties, and that free elections would be held to set up permanent governments. Russia promised that the Big Three Powers, and not the Soviet Union alone, would oversee the emergence of these free democratic nations.

Thus the political dominance of Russia in east-ern-central Europe was largely recognized. The United States and Britain would keep their word; would Russia? "Sombre indeed," exclaimed Churchill, "would be the fortunes of mankind if some awful schism arose between the Western democracies and the Russian Soviet Union. . . ." His words had prophetic force. All these important pledges respecting the freedom and autonomy of the eastern European nations Russia shortly honored in the breach.

It was Russian bad faith rather than Anglo-American generosity which ultimately made the Yalta agreements seem so unhappy. If Roosevelt could have foreseen that Japan would stand within a few days of defeat when Russia finally entered the Pacific War; if he could have foreseen that when victory was gained, Stalin and Molotov would revert to the surly suspicion toward all capitalist and socialist states which had marked their pre-war attitudes, he would have taken a different course. His concessions at the expense of China, without Chinese knowledge or consent, are par-ticularly hard to defend.

As early as March, 1945, the course of events in Rumania and Poland seemed to indicate that the Russians were determined to create subservient governments in eastern Europe in defiance of the Atlantic Charter and Yalta engagements. Robert

E. Sherwood and others tell us that Roosevelt would not have made his firm commitment, behind China's back, had he not been worn out at the end of the Conference and anxious to cut argument short. But his concessions, however unfortunate, had this measure of justification: MacArthur and other military advisers believed that the war would last much longer, and that a costly Russian effort would be needed to pin down the Japanese armies on the mainland of Asia. The Russian promise to help defeat Japan and to start twenty-five divisions eastward at once seemed to offer ground for generous treatment. Moreover, Stalin's intentions at the moment appeared highly honorable.

The stage was now set for the final act in the creation of an effective world union: the holding of a conference of fifty countries to perfect the United Nations Charter. Nobody could foresee the future development of eastern Europe. Nobody could predict the ultimate destiny of Germany, over whose treatment men were already quarreling; for Secretary Morgenthau had presented at the Second Quebec Conference a plan for reducing the Reich to a primitive stage of economy which the State Department combated with all its power. That plan, writes Secretary Hull, "angered me as much as anything that had happened during my career as Secretary of State"; and he and others procured its rejection. Germany would be demilitarized and many of her plants would be dismantled, but the best American and British experts knew that she could not be reduced to a mere agricultural country with a few small industries. Whatever the disputes as to a detailed European settlement, however, all men agreed that a world organization must be set in motion. It was unfortunate that Hull's ill health deprived him of the satisfaction of presiding over the crowning activities of his great design. But since Roosevelt was in any event expected to control the American delegation, which Stettinius headed, the resignation of the aged Secretary seemingly made little practical difference. Returning from Yalta in the early days of 1945, the President issued invitations for the historic gathering in San Francisco.

Then fell the heaviest blow of all. On April 12, the world was stunned by news of Roosevelt's sudden death. With victory in Europe practically won, and with the San Francisco Conference not a fortnight distant, the leader who had dominated the American scene for twelve years, and who had become the greatest figure in world affairs, was suddenly snatched away.

Yet the spirit of Roosevelt and Hull—their vibrant belief in world fellowship, their breadth of view, their optimism, their readiness to concede small points to gain great ends—was felt throughout the San Francisco Conference. As it began in the Opera House of that city, every voice of national opinion showed a realization that the fortunes of America were inextricably bound together with those of mankind, and that the boldest course would be the safest. Stalin, thinking better of his early plan of sending no important representative, dispatched Foreign Minister Molotov. Anthony Eden headed the British delegation. With prudent tolerance, Roosevelt had chosen a delegation which amply represented the Senate and the Republican party. Besides Hull (too ill to attend), it included Senator Vandenberg of Michigan, Representative Charles A. Eaton of New Jersey, and ex-Governor Harold E. Stassen of Minnesota, all Republicans; Senator Tom Connally of Texas and Representative Sol Bloom of New York, Democrats; and Dean Virginia C. Gildersleeve of Barnard College as spokesman for women. Special efforts had been made to educate American opinion, the Government sending out speakers, scattering pamphlets and articles, and inviting about a hundred organized groups to Washington to hear experts explain the Dumbarton Oaks Proposals.

With these proposals as basis, the San Francisco Conference showed more harmony than had been expected. Most of the disputes grew out of Russian attitudes. The revelation just before the Conference met of Roosevelt's consent to the Russian demand for three votes in the General Assembly caused much feeling, for it contravened the classic principle of one nation, one vote, in absolute equality. As soon as the Conference opened, a dispute between Russia on one side, America and Britain on the other, as to which of two rival claimants for power in Poland should be recognized, resulted in a deadlock which excluded Poland from the Conference. While the matter was undecided the Soviet Government coolly arrested negotiators from the opposition Polish regime who had gone to Moscow under safe conduct. Russia strenuously objected to the admission of Argentine delegates. The Latin-American nations supported their sister republic, however, and when the United States took their side Argentina won her place. As soon as regional agreements, such as the Pan-American defense arrangement just embodied in the Act of Chapultepec, came up for examination, the Soviet Union manifested a highly suspicious attitude. Only after much bickering, with the American nations presenting a firm front, was a formula devised which reconciled regional agreements with the all-inclusive United Nations framework. In dealing with colonial possessions Russia, which had no detached holdings, pressed for more radical steps toward immediate liberation than the other powers were willing to take, and again a compromise had to be arranged.

Finally, and most importantly, a bitter contest developed over the veto power claimed by the Big Five. The compromise which Roosevelt had devised in the "Yalta Formula" was announced shortly before the Conference. It divided actions taken by the Security Council into two types, "procedural" and "substantive"; stated that procedural matters could be decided by *any* seven out of the eleven votes; and required that all or practically all substantive issues (some matters of pacific settlement excepted) should be decided by seven votes *including* each of the five members of the Council. The Yalta scheme was based on the assumption that effective action to safeguard peace was impossible unless all the Big Five agreed on it. About forty-five of the lesser nations, aggressively led by Herbert V. Evatt of Australia, immediately attacked the Yalta compromise. They demanded that the veto be limited to enforcement action by the Security Council. Russia, on the other hand, wished the veto given the very widest application, demanding the right to use it even in stopping Council debate. The United States and Great Britain took a firm stand against the Soviet Union on this point, declaring that preliminary discussion of any dispute must be absolutely unfettered; and backed by the smaller nations, they won their contention that it must always be possible to bring up vexatious issues for debate and thus focus world

opinion upon them. At the same time, America and
Britain insisted that substantive action (investigation and enforcement) must be subject to the veto.
The final solution was theoretically satisfactory—
but Russia was soon to violate its spirit by a gross
abuse of the veto.

After two months of work, on June 25 the delegates by unanimous vote approved the Charter of
the United Nations. This set up three great main
agencies: a General Assembly, which was to serve
as a parliamentary sounding-board in expressing
the ideas of all nations, and in which each member-
state was to have one vote; a Security Council,
entrusted with "primary responsibility for the
maintenance of international peace and security,"
in which the United States, Great Britain, Russia,
China, and France were to be permanent members, while six other nations were to be elected
for two-year terms by a two-thirds vote of the
General Assembly; and an Economic and Social
Council, which was to promote higher standards
of living and full employment, solve international
problems in the cultural, health, social, and economic fields, and promote universal respect for
fundamental human rights. This third agency,
which had not existed in the old League, might
eventually (men hoped) become the most important of all. Provision was made for an international
police force, to be at the disposal of the Security

Council, and to be managed in part by a Military Staff Committee; but time proved that it was more difficult to create this arm than had been expected. The Charter provided that a number of fields of specialized activity should be covered by *ad hoc* international organizations, set up by intergovernmental agreements. Among these organizations, already existing or soon to be formed, were the International Labor Organization, the International Refugee Organization, the International Trade Organization, the Food and Agriculture Organization, and the United Nations Educational, Scientific, and Cultural Organization (UNESCO).

So strongly was American sentiment enlisted in favor of the Charter that prompt ratification was certain. The Senate Foreign Relations Committee reported the document without amendment, twenty members voting for it while only Hiram Johnson stood opposed. The final Senate action, taken July 28, 1945, was almost unanimous, 82 to 2.

ONE epoch in the history of American foreign relations had ended; another had begun. If any doubt of the fact remained in the United States, it was dispelled nine days later. President Truman had issued an official proclamation of Allied victory in Europe on May 9, 1945. Japan alone remained to be overcome. On August 6, a single B-29 winged its way above Hiroshima, and just after twelve

noon dropped a small bomb which exploded over
the city. Observers in the plane, smitten by a flash
of blinding intensity, saw "a giant pillar of purple
fire, ten thousand feet high, shooting skyward with
enormous speed"; and it had barely reached the
zenith when "there came shooting out of the top
a giant mushroom that increased the height of the
pillar to a total of 45,000 feet." Below these gigantic geysers of flame, smoke, and dust, soon reaching 60,000 feet into the stratosphere, Hiroshima
lay shattered, nearly a third of its population of
340,000 dead or stricken.

In the atomic bomb, developed at a cost of billions of dollars, America had perfected a weapon
which made a powerful and vigilant world organization for the preservation of peace a necessity if
civilization were to endure and grow.

Looking back over the span of thirty years since
Woodrow Wilson had committed himself to the
idea of a League for collective international security, Americans could trace a mingled record of
successes and failures in the sphere of world affairs.
They could take pride in the idealism exhibited in
the Washington Naval Conference, the Kellogg-
Briand Peace Pact, the Good Neighbor Policy, and
the Hoover-Stimson Non-Recognition Doctrine.
They could rejoice in the steadily growing amity
of the Pan-American family and the English-
speaking family. At the same time they had much

to regret. The rejection of the League was a sorry
chapter in the national record. The rampant isolationism under Harding and Coolidge, expressed in
such indefensible acts as the refusal to join the
World Court, was highly deplorable. The high
tariffs of 1921 and 1930, the narrow-minded and
selfish handling of the war debts, the blind Neutrality Acts of the mid-thirties, were blots on the
American shield. Much of this had now been
sponged away in blood and tears, and a new record
could be begun.

Peace by no means brought the world the general concord for which it hoped. The Western
powers and Russia had fundamentally different
ideologies; harmony between them had been purchased only by wartime concessions on the part of
Roosevelt and Churchill, which, when the guns
ceased and old suspicions and antagonisms returned, seemed to have been wasted. Some of these
concessions, as we have seen, had been made at
the expense of the Polish republic, and that nation
took over a wide area of Germany, including Bres-
lau and Stettin, to compensate herself. Russia regarded this arrangement as sound and permanent;
the Western nations regarded it as unjust and temporary. The demands of the Soviet Union for
reparations from Germany, reaching (in addition
to vast seizures of material) ten billion dollars,
were rejected by the West as impossibly high;

while the United States and Britain also opposed the Russian insistence on payment from current production, which would have given Moscow a stranglehold on the German economy. For her part, Russia regarded with mistrust the exclusive control of the Ruhr by first British and then Anglo-American authorities. Most disturbing of all, to the Western democracies, was the refusal of Russia to honor her pledge of free elections and uncontrolled governments in the small nations stretching from Poland to Rumania and Bulgaria. All of them, including even liberal Czechoslovakia, lapsed in time under Communist dictatorships which the majority of the people did not want. It became necessary for the Western nations to take earnest steps to protect Iran, Turkey, and Greece against Russian pressure. As the tension between Communism and capitalist enterprise grew, associates of Roosevelt recalled that before his death he had shown disillusionment with the Russian Government and had declared privately that American attitudes toward Russia would have to be changed.

Harmony had no existence in China, where a wasting civil war between the Nationalist Government and the Communists defied all American efforts to arrange a compromise. Harmony was sadly wanting in India as Great Britain moved in 1947 to give the varied races and faiths of that subcontinent full independence. Even in the Western Hemisphere difficulties continued. Argentina, yet ruled by Fascist groups, yet jealous of the loans and lend-lease obtained from the United States by Brazil, and yet resentful of outside criticism, remained a truculent member of the American family.

The United Nations was soon hopefully on its feet, its General Assembly giving all countries an opportunity to voice their grievances and apprehensions, and its Security Council dealing energetically with large problems. But it had to begin its work in a jangling, confused, and sorely distressed world, which was undergoing profound economic and social upheavals, and which was certain to witness tremendous changes in political equilibrium. It was soon evident, too, that it was handicapped by the serious differences between the Soviet Union and its satellites on one side, and the democratic nations on the other, and that much time and effort would be required to establish it firmly. The American people and Government would not stint their share of this effort.

The United States, like the rest of the world, had thrown away a priceless opportunity after the First World War. By paying a terrible price in lives, money, and the irremediable waste of its natural resources, it had lifted itself out of the depths of the ensuing perils. In doing so it had gained in wisdom and maturity; and perhaps the best single element in the hopes of mankind for the future lay in the realism and sense of responsibility with which nearly 150,000,000 Americans, so much the richest, strongest, and best-schooled people on the planet, were at last facing their duties as citizens of what Wendell Willkie had called One World.

BIBLIOGRAPHICAL NOTE

A VARIETY of publications have been issued by the
State Department upon American foreign policy since
1930. Of these the *Department of State Bulletins* and
the *Press Releases* contain valuable documentary material; while the volumes of *Foreign Affairs*, issued at
somewhat irregular intervals, will eventually supply
what materials can properly be given to the general
public. Various collections of papers have also been
issued by private agencies. Of these the annual volumes
of *Documents on American Foreign Relations*, edited
at first by L. M. Goodrich and later by L. M. Goodrich and M. J. Carroll, had reached their sixth volume
in 1945. The British counterpart, *Documents on International Affairs*, edited by various hands for the
Royal Institute of International Affairs (popularly
called Chatham House), is equally indispensable.
Valuable documentary material and analyses by experts are available in the monthly issue by the Car-
negie Endowment for International Peace, *International Conciliation*. The New York *Times* made a
special feature of the verbatim text of important
speeches by world leaders as well as diplomatic
documents.

Beginning in the 1930's it became possible to study
public opinion more or less scientifically through the

Gallup and other polls. The results are to be found in files of the *Public Opinion Quarterly*, and in *Opinion News*, issued by the National Opinion Research Center. The quarterly *Foreign Affairs*, published by the Council on Foreign Relations, is full of expert articles; so is the bi-monthly *International Affairs*, issued by the Royal Institute. While the *Congressional Record* is difficult to use because of its bulk, its debates are indispensable. Special attention is paid to international relations by the *Manchester Guardian Weekly*, London *Spectator*, *New Republic*, and *Nation*. The semi-monthly *Foreign Policy Reports* of the Foreign Policy Association are often illuminating. Good annual summaries of international events are available in the *Yearbook* of the *Encyclopaedia Britannica*, the *American Year Book*, and *New International Year Book*.

The fullest general surveys of the period are to be found in the latest revised editions of Thomas A. Bailey, *A Diplomatic History of the American People* (1947); Samuel Flagg Bemis, *A Diplomatic History of the United States* (1942); and R. W. Van Alstyne, *American Diplomacy in Action: a Series of Case Studies* (1944). A broad survey with much firsthand material is Sumner Welles, *The Time for Decision* (1944). Efforts to state varying views of the fundamental principles of American foreign policy may be found in Walter Lippmann, *U. S. Foreign Policy: Shield of the Republic* (1943); Ross Hoffman, *Durable Peace: a Study in American National Policy* (1944); Nathaniel Peffer, *America's Place in the World* (1945); and Hugh Gibson, *The Road to Foreign Policy* (1944).

Latin-American relations have been studied in a large number of works, most of them more journalistic than historical. Ray Josephs presents an outline of wartime and post-war developments in *Latin America: Continent in Crisis* (1948). Carleton Beals and others have explained *What the South Americans Think of Us* (1945). J. Fred Rippy has dealt expertly with *South America and Hemisphere Defense* (1941), and W. H. C. Laves and various associates with *Inter-American Solidarity* (1941). By far the best book on the Monroe Doctrine is Dexter Perkins's brilliant summation of a larger three-volume study, *Hands Off: a History of the Monroe Doctrine* (1941). The most difficult problem in the Pan-American sphere is expertly analyzed in C. H. Haring's *Argentina and the United States* (1941). Excellent general surveys are available in Samuel Flagg Bemis, *The Latin American Policy of the United States* (1943), G. H. Stuart's *Latin America and the United States* (fourth edition, 1943), and Hubert Herring, *America and the Americas: an Appraisal and a Forecast* (1944). Professor Arthur P. Whitaker has edited an annual volume of *Inter-American Affairs* and has published an interesting book on *The United States and South America: the Northern Republics* (1948).

One of the most penetrating books ever written on Canadian affairs, J. Bartlett Brebner's *North Atlantic Triangle* (1945), discusses historically, as the subtitle indicates, "the interplay of Canada, the United States, and Great Britain." The older volume by H. L. Keenleyside, *Canada and the United States* (1929), is dryly factual but accurate. H. F. Angus has edited an illuminating volume called *Canada and Her Great*

Neighbor (1938); while a keen-minded journalist, John McCormac, informs Americans why they cannot neglect the Dominion, in *Canada: America's Problem* (1940). *The Unguarded Frontier* (1942) is by a distinguished Canadian scholar, E. W. McInnis.

The basic recent book on Far Eastern relations, A. W. Griswold's *The Far Eastern Policy of the United States* (1938), is both readable and scholarly. A subsequent volume of much merit is T. A. Bisson's *America's Far Eastern Policy* (1945). Nathaniel Peffer's *Basis for Peace in the Far East* (1942) and Owen Lattimore's *Solution in Asia* (1945) are both by experts, and both reject old style imperialism emphatically. S. K. Hornbeck's *The United States and the Far East* (1942) is valuable.

Most treatments of American-Russian relations suffer from bias in one direction or the other. Foster Rhea Dulles has written an entertaining and accurate account of these relations from the beginning in *The Road to Teheran* (1944); its brevity makes it necessarily somewhat sketchy. The sociologist P. A. Sorokin brought out in 1944 a cheerful view of *Russia and the United States*, while the next year a Russian scholar-refugee, David J. Dallin, took a much gloomier view in *The Big Three: the United States, Britain, Russia*. John R. Deane has contributed a revealing study of *The Strange Alliance: the Story of Our Wartime Cooperation with Russia* (1947). The second volume of Max Beloff's *The Foreign Policy of Soviet Russia, 1929–41* (1949) covers the years after 1935. It is supplemented by A. Rossi's *Deux Ans d'Alliance Germano–Soviétique, 1939–41* (1949). Martin Ebon's *World Communism Today* (1948) is an able summary of the strength and weakness of Communism throughout the globe.

A classic work of perdurable literary and historical value, Winston Churchill's *The Gathering Storm* (1948), the first volume of his memoirs of the Second World War, is indispensable to all students of the period. Also indispensable, but in a different way, are the two volumes of Cordell Hull's *Memoirs* (1948), the first volume coming down to 1941, and the second covering the war years. Minutely detailed, they cover every aspect of the State Department's work from the beginning of the Roosevelt Administrations down to Mr. Hull's resignation because of ill health at the end of 1944. All the Secretary's policies are defended with an elaborate array of facts. The book is dull in style, but is a tremendous storehouse of information. Somewhat more lively, and highly illuminating throughout, is Henry L. Stimson's *On Active Service in Peace and War* (1948), written with the collaboration of McGeorge Bundy. Mr. Stimson's trenchant memoirs after 1940 deal mainly with War Department affairs, but throw many sidelights on international relations. Robert Sherwood's *Roosevelt and Hopkins: an Intimate History* (1948) also throws much light on wartime diplomacy, while Joseph F. Brynes's volume, *Speaking Frankly* (1947), justifies its title. The second volume of Churchill's memoirs, *Their Finest Hour*, again of classic quality, appeared in 1949.

A large body of works appeared in 1942–46 on the organization of peace and the proper basis for the United Nations. While most of them were of but transient value, they all throw light on the national psychology at the time. The more important titles include

Herbert Hoover and Hugh Gibson, *The Problems of Lasting Peace* (1942); J. M. Jones, *A Modern Foreign Policy for the United States* (1944); Kenneth W. Colegrove, *The American Senate and World Peace* (1944); and Henry M. Wriston, *Strategy of Peace*. An eloquent plea for the abatement of national sovereignty and founding of a world government was written by Emery Reves in *The Anatomy of Peace*, and another, borrowing force from the atomic bomb, by Norman Cousins in *Modern Man Is Obsolete* (both 1945). The actual operation of the new world organization is critically analyzed by Herbert Vere Evatt in *The United Nations* (1948).

Among books of the war period which combated isolationism effectively, Wendell L. Willkie's hard-hitting *One World* (1943), Sumner Welles's *The Time for Decision* (1944), which contained much interesting material on his observations as Under Secretary of State and roving diplomatist, and Walter Lippmann's *U. S. War Aims* (1944) all had a large circulation. The controversial subject of relations with Spain finds interesting discussion in *Wartime Mission in Spain, 1942–45*, by Carlton J. H. Hayes, the American Ambassador (1945), and in *Ambassador on Special Mission*, by Viscount Templewood (Sir Samuel Hoare), the British Ambassador (1946); both excellent books. Anglo–American relations are fully described in a number of books, of which Crane Brinton's admirable summary, *The United States and Britain* (1945), deserves special mention. For the study of relations with Japan just before war broke out two volumes by the American and British Ambassadors are extremely useful; Joseph C. Grew's diffuse but shrewd *Ten Years in Japan* (1944), and Sir Robert Craigie's more compact and penetrating *Behind the Japanese Mask* (1945). North African affairs were treated while the subject was still hot in three interesting books, Leon Marchal's *Vichy: Two Years of Deception* (1944), Kenneth Pendar's *Adventure in Diplomacy* (1945), and R. Renée Pierre-Gosset's *Conspiracy in Algiers, 1942–43* (1945); all three decidedly partisan. D. W. Brogan has written a thoughtful book on *French Personalities and Problems* (1947). An expert and fairly impartial summing up has been furnished by a careful scholar, W. L. Langer, in *Our Vichy Gamble* (1947). The memoirs of General Dwight D. Eisenhower, *Crusade in Europe* (1948), give a soldier's view of relations with Giraud and Darlan.

Walter Millis's *This Is Pearl!* (1947) is an admirable study of the events immediately preceding Pearl Harbor, concise, accurate, and dramatic. His volume *Why Europe Fights* (1941) also deserves warm commendation. The best summing up of the revelations in the Nuremberg Trials is to be found in Peter Calvocoressi, *Nuremberg* (1947). In *The Price of Power* (1948) Hanson Baldwin expertly analyzes the problems of political and military strategy faced by the United States in the new atomic age.

INDEX

Air power, expansion of, 214 f.
Albania, attack on, 179
A. F. of L., resolution vs. Japan, 135
Anglo-American war cooperation, 254 ff.
Anglo-French alliance, 180 ff.
Anglo-French Purchasing Mission, 200 f.
Anglo-American naval agreement, 68; abrogated by Hitler, 181
Anti-Comintern Pact, 73 f.
Appeasement, 106, 112, 152 ff.; shift to resistance, 177
Argentina, 268, 281 ff.; Nazi organizations, 167; U. S. attitude toward, 283 ff.; and the Chapultepec conference, 284 ff.; hostilities vs. the Axis, 285 f.; and the United Nations, 306
Ashton-Gwatkin, F. T., 177
Atlantic Charter, 248, 252
Atom bomb, 309 f.
Austria, Nazi occupation, of, 137 ff.

Baker, Newton D., 52
Baldwin, Stanley, 99
Baltic States, 189
Bases, destroyers exchanged for, 219 f.
Bases, naval and air, lease of, 217, 250
Beard, Charles A., 51
Ball, Joseph H., 291
Belgium, invasion, 213 f.
Berle, A. A., Jr., 33, 251

Bloom, Sol, 305
Blum, Leon, 99, 107, 145 f., 148
Bohemia and Moravia, 178
Bonnet, Georges, 13, 148 f.
Borah, W. E., 23
Bowers, Claude, 97
Brazil, 268, 281; Fascism and Nazism in, 168 f.
Bretton Woods conference, 294 f.
Broun, Heywood, 192
Burke-Wadsworth Act, 219
Butler, Nicholas Murray, 203
Byrnes, James F., 195, 297

Caffery, Jefferson, 28
Cairo conference, 263
Canada, and the U. S., 37 ff.; vs. the Axis threat, 218
Canadian-American Defense Board, 249
Canton, air raids, 133 f.
Caribbean republics, 268
Casablanca conference, 256
"Cash-and-carry," 102 f., 196
Central Europe, USSR in, 302
Cespedes, Carlos de, 28
Chaco war, *see* Gran Chaco
Chamberlain, Neville, 75, 99, 147; peace talks with Hitler, 152 ff.; "peace in our time," 157; Birmingham speech, 1939, 177; Birmingham speech *re* Czechoslovakia, 180; speech *re* Poland, 180 f.
Chamberlin, W. H., 193
Chapultepec, Act of, 306
Chapultepec conference, 284 ff.
Chautemps, Camille, 99, 148

323